Spiritual Burnout

Spiritual Burnout

by

MALCOLM SMITH

A Division of Harrison House, Inc.
Tulsa, Oklahoma

Cover photo: Scott Miller

4th Printing
Over 27,000 in Print

Spiritual Burnout
ISBN 0-89274-517-7
Copyright © 1988 by Malcolm Smith
Malcolm Smith Ministries
Box 29747
San Antonio, TX 78229

Published by Honor Books
A Division of Harrison House Publishers
P. O. Box 35035
Tulsa, Oklahoma 74153

DEDICATION

To my wife Ginger for the many hours spent in editing the manuscript and her practical spiritual insight and constant encouragement, whose name, in my opinion, should be on the cover with mine.

CONTENTS

Spiritual Burnout

Chapter 1

EVIDENCES OF

SPIRITUAL BURNOUT

We sat in a cafe in the Mayfair area of London. Outside, the fog was settling in on the late November afternoon. The gloom outside matched the dark despair that registered on the face of my friend across the table. I had sat down with Jack, full of all that had been happening in our recent work in Africa . . . but I soon backed off when I saw his total disinterest and depression.

"Why do you preach love, Malcolm?" He looked at me over his tea cup, his face showing the anger that was reflected in his voice. "Why don't you preach on doctrine? Then we can do what all Christians do best: argue, divide and say God told us to start another church!"

I was surprised at the sudden outburst and the cynical tone of his words. I had not seen Jack in many months. He had been the pastor of a successful church in Scotland and was a well-known convention speaker, not only in the United Kingdom but also in the United States and Australia.

It had taken me off guard when I received his call a few months before. Jack said he had resigned the ministry and was now selling insurance . . . said he needed to get out of the pastorate to become the husband and the father he had neglected to be. "I woke up one day and realized my boys were growing up, and I hardly knew them."

Passing through London en route from Johannesburg to New York, I set aside time for a visit, but was not prepared for the dark cloud that hung over him. This was not the man I had known over the years . . . a man filled with excitement and vision, always discussing his latest program for church growth or something new he had seen in the Scriptures.

In the last two hours, he had injected his negative outlook into every subject we had discussed. Anything I shared, concerning God's work and the ministry, only drew sarcastic remarks. His last comment was almost violent.

The previous evening I had spoken in a local church on the love command of Jesus. Jack had obviously been thinking about it all day. He looked across the table, his face sending a mixture of signals . . . disgust, anger, apology and, most of all, despair.

Except for the sound of the tea being poured into his empty cup, there was silence. "I mean it, Malcolm. You preach love, but you know that no one will ever *do* what you say! I watched them last night. They agree with you, nod their heads and shout praises to the Lord; they line up to shake your hand and say how they were blessed. And before they get home, they are gossiping, fighting and betraying their friends. But bless God, they don't smoke or drink wine!" He spat out the last words with venom.

He looked down for a moment and when he looked up, I saw a tired man, weary with life and at present in deep despair. Quietly, he said, "This is why I quit, Malcolm. I could have rearranged my schedule to give more time to my family. That was just a good excuse. The real reason is . . ." He stopped and stared moodily at the thickening fog outside. ". . . the real reason is, it doesn't work. Does it, Malcolm? It's all talk and going through religious motions, but no one is changed!

"There were times when I felt like a drug pusher. The congregation paid me to give them their regular injections to convince them they ought to keep trying to be good Christians for another week! And they went on their way believing that, this time, things would be better. But we know nothing will change because it doesn't work!" His voice was husky with a sob in it now, but he still spoke with anger.

"That is what I had to face up to last year: I was a minister and I preached the Gospel, but most of the New Testament, when it came to living it, was out of my reach. I just kept preaching and hoped no one would notice that my life was as empty as theirs.

"You were right last night, Malcolm. Jesus left us with one command: **. . . love one another** (John 15:17 NAS). I agree that He called us to live in the here and now with divine love, but I came to the conclusion that I could no longer continue to preach it while seeing no evidence of it actually working.

"One day about a year ago, I realized just how sick I was of the empty religious lives of my congregation, sick of the masks we all wore . . . myself included. So you see, I meant what I said. If you are going to stay in the Church, then preach doctrine and you will fuel the reason these people stay around.

"I mean, at least, let's enjoy a bad scene! Preach doctrine, attack everyone who doesn't agree with you, and the people will love you. Find all the dirt you can in the life of the fellow who disagrees with you and let everyone know about it — people will believe you are so holy you must have all the truth. Everyone will think that you are an apostle with a new revelation, and you will be able to start another church!" He turned and stared into the now dark street through the misty window of the cafe.

9

Jack is one more who has joined the increasing number of casualties who have fallen exhausted by the wayside, spiritually burned out.

Norman is a bright-eyed young manager of a grocery store in the Midwest. Whenever we talk of the things of God, his bright eyes grow misty and he turns away. At times his voice has a sob in it.

After graduating from Bible school, he became the pastor of a small group of people who wanted to have all that God had for them. God blessed and they grew rapidly. Then came the bitter arguments between him and some of the elders; there was talk of his right-hand man breaking away with half of the congregation. One morning, Norman packed his bags and left town.

As we chatted by the pet supplies, he opened his heart to me. He said he had realized he had no spiritual strength to draw from, his reservoir was empty and he could not handle the pressure that went with pastoring a growing church.

In that state of exhaustion, he became disgusted with the vicious back-biting and back-stabbing in the church — the very church he had built! He shook his head sadly, "Malcolm, there is more love in a bar than in the Church!"

I see Phil every time I am in Houston. He is an insurance agent, middle-aged with hair greying at the temples. Having spent most of his life pastoring a church in California, he is trying to find success in the insurance business.

Most of his waking moments had been spent building a very successful church and speaking around the country in large spiritual life conventions. Over the years he lost touch with his family; his wife grew cold and distant. Believing they had stolen her husband away from her, she resented God and the church. One day, he found himself having a passionate affair with his young secretary.

He told me sadly, "All my work for God exhausted me. When temptation came, I had no strength to resist! Quite honestly, I couldn't believe it when I realized I had become involved with another woman. The ministry had become a business, and God was very far away." When his wife heard of the affair, she walked out and divorced him.

In his cubby-hole office, with tears in his eyes, he looked at me across his desk and said, "If only things had been different! The most frightening thing about it all is, if you are going to be successful in the ministry in today's world, I don't know any other way to do it!

"Any successful minister I know is running close to the line with his family. Most of them are empty on the inside — just hoping no one will find out! I know . . . I have talked with them."

Spiritual burnout runs parallel to what is happening in the secular world. There the term *burnout* has been coined to describe the condition of the person who has become mentally and emotionally exhausted in his reach for success in his field.

Dr. Herbert Freudenberger describes the person who has burned out as, "Someone in a state of fatigue or frustration brought about by devotion to a cause, a way of life, or relationship, that failed to produce the expected reward."[1] The man or woman who does not reach for the top will never suffer from burnout; it is a condition found only among those who want the best!

Spiritual burnout is not something that only happens to ministers. When ministers burn out, they get unwanted publicity and, sometimes, even headlines in the local newspaper. But we are seeing an epidemic of drop outs from church membership rolls; not the Easter and Christmas members, but the exemplary, enthusiastic church workers. Usually, their leaving is sparked by a quarrel with another worker or hurt and anger at not being given the recognition they feel they deserve.

Suddenly, they are no more. Now on Sundays, they sit at home, soured and resentful at whoever it was that caused the upheaval. Some have thought about what happened. They have realized that all they had believed about the power to live the Christian life had failed when they needed it the most. Incredibly, their faith had been short-circuited by another human being not doing things the way they wanted.

Not everyone leaves the Church when they burn out. A few months ago, I interviewed a number of members of a pentecostal church in a Chicago suburb. They all agreed that the Christian life is not what it used to be. All I spoke with were quick to tell me of the way the Spirit had moved in the rented pool hall on Second and Main when the church had started 15 years before.

Over the years, a number of the members have left. "The Lord was pruning us, getting rid of the dead wood," they told me. The congregation appears to be the custodian of a memory, seeking every Sunday morning, week after week, to relive the past through the monotonous singing of the same old songs. Once the songs had expressed an inner fire, but today they reminded me of sad dirges sung at the funeral of a church that refuses to be buried.

The members did not leave their church. No, they settled, instead, for something a lot less than the vision God had planted in their hearts when they first came to Christ.

One of the saddest days of my ministry was in 1963 on a preaching tour in South Wales. I visited the churches that had been birthed out of the Welsh Revival in 1904. But today, they are burned out. They are like the cool ashes in a fireplace, reminders of last night's fire.

The saddest of all was the church where Evan Roberts had prayed the night the great revival had begun. On the wall of the little chapel is a plaque telling the world that on this spot Evan Roberts prayed and brought revival to the world.

If the plaque had not been there, I would never have known that this was where the rivers of life had broken into the world in 1904 . . . for the spiritual temperature in the building was almost zero.

That marvelous night, some of the members had been kneeling beside Evan Roberts and recited to me a minute by minute account of the events that had transpired. Those dear people were tour guides in a spiritual museum! Whatever had energized them 60 years before was now only a memory; all that was left was a monument and that plaque on the wall.

I came away asking, "Lord Jesus, why? Why did a congregation, graced with one of the greatest moves of the Spirit in this generation, burn out in less than 60 years?" While traveling the world since then, I have had to ask that same question many times.

We have all heard of the thousands who have come to Christ in foreign lands. But not all of us know that many times, within a few short months, there is little evidence that anything ever happened! Why?

To say the evangelist didn't lay a good foundation is to deliberately avoid the embarrassing facts. I know a number of these evangelists . . . the Word was preached and the signs did follow the proclamation of the Gospel. But something happened — or failed to happen — to the new converts. Today, they sit in their huts and remember the weeks when God was so real.

Like Cleopas and his friend on their way back to Emmaus, they had heard Jesus, seen His works and were ready to throw their lives away for Him. Now He was dead as far as they knew, and it seemed they had literally thrown away their lives for a dead dream.

Some shake their heads and say that the devil won a victory. If that is the answer, it only raises more questions. Jesus ascended victorious over all the powers of hell! He said He would build His Church and the gates of hell would not prevail against it. Something is wrong if the devil can blow it away so easily.

Why are people burning out, dropping out or settling down to the boredom of what is called "church" today? Where shall we look to stop the swelling river of believers who are being swept out of our ranks?

Some say we should pray more. I do not discount prayer, but I have discovered that many of those praying are themselves prime candidates for spiritual exhaustion! Whatever causes spiritual burnout is deeper than lack of prayer.

Others say we suffer from lack of faith. "We must build our faith, feed our spirits with the Word . . . and we will be invincible." I agree the Church is woefully short on faith and in desperate need to return to the life that is in the Word of God. However, some of the most tragic cases of burnout I have met have come from among those who claim to understand faith.

Janet came to me after a meeting, tears flowing freely. Between sobs, she shared how she had been believing God for her little daughter's healing. Every waking hour, she confessed the Scriptures that pertained to healing; if she woke in the night, she immediately continued to recite the promises of God.

She was afraid that, should she forget or fail to confess the healing, it would keep her daughter in sickness. She even thought to fast from sleep in order to keep a 24-hour vigil. By the time she came to me, she was a spiritual, emotional, nervous and physical wreck. A burnout in every way.

I believe in healing, and I also believe that faith is the channel by which all of His blessings flow to us. But whatever Janet had been taught or how ever she had interpreted what she had been taught, it contained the deadly seed that frustrates the great works of God in a believer's life.

Neil and I had gotten to know each other when I ministered at the church he attended. On each visit I fellowshipped with him and his wife, Melissa. I was surprised when he wrote and told me Melissa had been diagnosed as having leukemia. He asked me to join him and many others in prayer for her healing.

Only a few weeks later, she was dead and, as I was in the vicinity, I went to the funeral. Horrified, standing by the coffin, I heard Neil solemnly say, "I killed Melissa . . . we all did! If I had had more faith, she would have been healed. If all of you had exercised more faith, she would be alive today." Sour and bitter, Neil finally left the church.

An extreme case? Maybe . . . but I knew that one more time I had come up against the one element that is present every time I meet a case of spiritual burnout.

Hardly a meeting goes by without someone coming to me and expressing their questions and concerns . . . many of which they keep hidden from their fellow believers. Passing through their lives as I do, it appears to be safe to share with me.

Jackie joined me for breakfast while I was conducting meetings in a Midwestern city. She and her husband had been members of a mainline denominational church since they had moved to the city some years before. A hunger for God had been born in their hearts, and they were drawn to the church where our meetings were being held.

"I suppose I am being unthankful and asking for too much," she smiled nervously as she spoke, "but I sometimes ask myself about the Christian life. I mean, is this it? Is this all there is? Don't misunderstand me . . . it's so much better than anything we ever had before. God is real to me, but honestly, Malcolm, what we call church is not much more than a religious club — and I guess that's okay."

She hesitated before saying, "I get so frustrated sometimes. Did Jesus die and rise again to be the founder of a club where we all try to be like Him . . . sing in the choir, drive our kids to concerts, send them to the church school, listen to pep talks every Sunday and say 'Amen' in the right place and go bowling with church people on Tuesday nights? Malcolm, if this is what Jesus is all about, He's very boring!"

As she stood back, red in the face, I knew here was another potential burnout victim — unless she got some answers. She was the voice of many who felt the same way, but would never openly express it.

What is this deadly poison that is spreading through the Church? We have avoided facing the problem, pretended it doesn't exist or blamed the devil — and then, embarrassed, we have shunned those exhausted, burned-out believers who have dropped out of the Church. But the problem is there and will not go away. In fact, it is becoming an epidemic.

One morning, as I was walking in the Catskill Mountains in New York, I witnessed an unforgettable sight. I was resting, sitting on a rock by an algae-covered pool. Lazily, while mosquitoes engaged in a never-ending dance close to the surface, I watched the dragon flies dart between the reeds. A frog sunned himself on a partially submerged rock out in the center of the pool.

Suddenly, I was wide awake. Something was happening to the frog. Before my eyes, it collapsed . . . not falling over, but deflating like a balloon with a slow leak. It finally lay in a dreadful crumpled heap of frog skin; its insides were completely gone!

It was only then that I saw the killer. A giant water bug had bitten the frog, injecting it with a substance that dissolved its insides. Then he had proceeded to suck out the inside of the frog, leaving the skin like an empty grocery bag on the rock.

Many believers are like the frog . . . there is something sucking the life and vitality out of them. They are spiritually drained, their thoughts have become negative and cynical. Bitter and resentful, God seems very far away. They are spiritually burned out.

Footnotes

[1]Herbert Freudenberger and Geraldine Richelson, *Burn-Out: The High Cost of High Achievement* (New York: Doubleday, 1981).

Chapter 2

THE DEADLY BROTH

OF LEGALISM

When the prophet Elisha went to visit with some students of the Scriptures in Gilgal, there was a famine in the land of Israel.

It came time to eat and, while the pot was boiling, one of the students went out to find some vegetables to make a stew. Because there were no vegetables to be had from the farms, the student had to forage in the wild pastures around the community.

He found what he believed to be cucumbers. In actual fact, they were probably what was known as a "squirting cucumber" which, although it looked like the real vegetable, was poisonous.

The student returned and, elated that he had so quickly found enough food for everyone, began immediately to prepare the soup. Everyone saw the bowl of chopped pieces sitting on the table and thought they were seeing cucumbers.

The soup bubbled while Elisha taught; there was no smell to suggest that the broth was deadly. Of course, no one was looking for any symptom that would suggest anything was wrong. Why should they? One of their own had gathered and cooked the meal; and he, the chef, was himself going to eat it!

It wasn't until the food was in their mouths that someone recognized it was the taste of poison and death. He shouted out, "There is death in the pot!" Elisha's response was to take some meal and throw it into the liquid. Miraculously, the soup immediately became edible and no longer poisonous.

We are living in days of a spiritual famine; spiritual food is not readily available where we expect to find it. The spiritually hungry have to go and forage for whatever they can get, wherever they can get it.

For the most part, as they set out, they have no knowledge of the Scriptures, just a burning desire to know more of God. They are amazed to find how much seems to grow in the farmlands of Bible bookstores and the almost endless supply of "cucumbers" growing on the mountainsides of Christian radio and television.

The real harvest is in the tapes that seem to be growing everywhere! And always, there is the special speaker at the local charismatic meeting.

In this search, there is little or no analysis of what is being said or of the way the Scriptures are interpreted. If the speaker or writer mentions the name of Jesus or uses the Bible as the basis for what he says, then his message is accepted.

No one notices that, many times, speakers contradict one another! As in a famine, anything that looks like food for the spirit is grasped. If the pastor is born again and Spirit-filled, then anything that is said from the pulpit must surely be right. If the book is sold in a Christian bookstore, it must be from God!

Many pastors find studying the Bible difficult. Consequently, they have a hard time preparing a weekly sermon that contains spiritual food. They are on a constant search, picking up anything they can feed to their people. On Sundays, they come with their messages — and they might as well be carrying an armful of squirting cucumbers!

Bystanders will not notice that what is being said is going to hurt the listeners. Why should they? They trust their pastor and quite correctly assume that he is going to apply to himself what he is teaching.

On one occasion, when preaching in a town in Connecticut, we asked at the local gas station for the best restaurant in town. We were hungry and wanted to eat before the meeting. We were referred to "Joe's Kitchen."

Under normal circumstances, I would never have eaten there, but we were hungry and had little time to spare. That night, I rolled in my bed in agony with stomach pains; by morning, I was too weak to get out of bed.

We have returned to that town many times, but I would rather starve than cross the threshold of Joe's Kitchen! I recognized that the food I ate was responsible for my sickness and total weakness.

When people are spiritually sick and exhausted, we must first ask about their spiritual diet. Death usually begins in the pot from which they eat . . . in the food that is usually prepared by a sincere pastor or evangelist who is eating the same food himself. They will burn out together.

The problems in the Church today are not *primarily* lack of prayer, Bible study, faith or dedication. Our problem goes far deeper than any of these things. Something has made us so weak, we do not want to pray or read the Bible . . . all enthusiasm for the things of God has been sucked out of us.

What is it that makes the exercise of faith such a struggle when, in fact, it is the gateway to the eternal rest of God? Why is it that our enthusiastic dedications have grown cold to the point we are tired of making them? Why is it many believers have tired of studying their Bibles? Why do our great words of victory fail when we need them the most?

Believers are burning out and dropping away exhausted because of the spiritual food they have been eating. There is death in the pot!

It is an incontestable fact that the Good News of Jesus Christ does not and cannot spiritually exhaust the person who believes it. The Gospel is called, . . . **the whole message of this Life** (Acts 5:20 NAS), the message of . . . **eternal life** (John 6:68 NAS) that assures us that we have . . . **passed out of death into life** (1 John 3:14 NAS).

It brings us . . . **the peace of God, which surpasses all** (human) **comprehension** . . . (Phil. 4:7 NAS), . . . **joy inexpressible** . . . (1 Pet. 1:8 NAS) and gives us . . . **the love of God . . . poured out within our hearts through the Holy Spirit** (Rom. 5:5 NAS). These are not expressions that describe a person who is burned out, cynical, faint and weary.

The believer is tempted and will sometimes fall. He will experience times of darkness that can only be likened to the Valley of the Shadow of Death. There are times when he finds himself in near despair and might, indeed, feel like giving up. But he doesn't!

Paul described his life as a believer: . . . **Never far from death, yet here we are alive, always "going through it" yet never "going under." We know sorrow, yet our joy is inextinguishable** (2 Cor. 6:9,10 Phi). He doesn't "go under" because of the revelation of God that he has in Christ that is contained in the Gospel.

While a person is living by the truths of the Gospel, he cannot burn out! A person who has dropped exhausted does so because he has believed a distortion of the Gospel (which is no Gospel!), or because he has forgotten the heart of the Gospel he once believed and has been led astray.

That being the case, we can say that the best thing for such a person is to drop exhausted on the side of the road of life. If what he is believing is not the Truth, then the sooner its inability to give him spiritual life and health is made manifest, the better.

In studying the ministry of Jesus, it is significant that He not only taught Truth, but He also attacked error . . . and did so at every opportunity.

Because it was killing them, He came to deliver the people from what they had been believing.

Early in His ministry, Jesus announced what He had come to do:

"The Spirit of the Lord is upon Me, Because He anointed Me to preach the gospel to the poor.

"He has sent Me to proclaim release to the captives,

And recovery of sight to the blind,

To set free those who are downtrodden,

To proclaim the favorable year of the Lord."

Luke 4:18,19 NAS

These statements are usually interpreted as meaning that He came to deliver mankind from the results of the Fall, from sin, disease and bondage to the powers of darkness. His ministry was the implementation of that announcement; and His death, resurrection and ascension broke the power of everything that held mankind in bondage.

What is overlooked is that, in implementing that manifesto in His earthly ministry, He set out to deliver people from a certain belief system. It would be true to say that Jesus was engaged in a constant war with a belief system that was held by the religious sect called the Pharisees.

It is important that Jesus never crusaded against prostitutes, thieves, drunkards or the tax collectors (the closest Israel knew to organized crime). In fact, He made them His friends. His entire ministry was a crusade against the teaching of the Pharisees.

What was this belief system that called forth the strongest and angriest words of Jesus? The Pharisees called people to come to acceptance by God through their own good works; it was the message of acceptance by performance. It is this message that is at the heart of all religion, and it is what leaves people exhausted in their efforts to perform acceptably for God.

Webster defines the word religion as: "Piety, conscientiousness, scrupulousness, from *religare*, to bind back; *re-*, and *ligare*, to bind

21

together; a state of mind or way of life expressing love for and trust in God and one's will and effort to act according to the will of God, especially within a monastic order or community."[1]

Religion is binding oneself to the keeping of rules that govern conduct, rituals and formulas by which to approach God. It calls for the exercise of the devotee's will for complete obedience to its precepts. The reason for binding oneself is to please God and be accepted by Him.

Religion began in the Garden of Eden at the Fall of man. The first expression of man's fallen condition was to flee the presence of God and hide from Him in the trees. From that time on, man outside of Christ has been afraid of God. He expresses that fear in atheism, which is hoping that He isn't there; and in materialism, which is hiding from Him in the material things of life, hoping He will go away!

Religion is the ultimate expression of the same fear. It sees God as angry with mankind, and seeks ways to appease Him and get His attention. Every religion in the world is the result of the speculations of man's fallen mind as to the meaning of life, its origins and goal, the character of the deity as each sees Him, and what one must do to be acceptable to Him.

It is interesting that, in their foundations, all religions of the world are the same: they see God as distant, unfriendly and the giver of laws by which to approach Him. These laws are entrusted to the elite of the religion, usually in book form, who interpret the laws to the worshippers. All religion, wherever we find it, is the upward reach of man searching for a way to please the God of Whom he is so afraid.

The Greeks defined human love in the word *eros*, which in English expresses the idea: "I desire for myself the highest, best and most beautiful."

Eros is the womb where all of man's upward reaches toward God are conceived. All of the rules and rituals that he believes will please God, begin right here. It is also the foundation of man's belief concerning the nature of God.

Eros is the highest and most beautiful emotion in man, reaching only for the best, drawing him ever up and away from the lowest towards the highest. It is only natural that, when the mind of fallen man defines God, he says, "God is the ultimate *Eros.*"

It is only one more step then to say that God only wants the most beautiful people, the best of mankind, those who have reached and attained the highest plane of life possible for a human to reach.

Religion is the defining of a ladder that guarantees acceptance by God when one has climbed to the top rung. It claims to be the revelation of the path up the mountain to the dizzy heights of perfection, and the familiarity with deity that goes along with it.

Built into this system of belief is pride. The climber of the ladder believes he has the only set of rules that finally pleases God, and so he looks at others as having less value than himself. He also feels it his duty to destroy all those who do not have the rules and will not receive them from him.

Eros is the basis of all religious wars, whether on the fields of battle or in the halls of theology. *Eros* always draws circles around itself, excluding all except those who have bound themselves to the keeping of the revealed rules.

The Pharisees' expression of religion was the most evil of all because of its subtlety. In its origins, the movement was built on the Word of God which, to hear its objectives, one finds difficult to fault.

A Pharisee was one who had dedicated himself to the keeping of the Law of Moses, called the *Torah* (the first five books of the Bible) in the Hebrew language. Their dedicatory oath was called, "taking the yoke of the *Torah*." From that day, they saw themselves as set apart to God, to His Law and to each other. They were a closed circle into which only the devout were welcomed, a circle in which they were separated from the world of sinners outside.

In actual fact, the demands of the Law were simple: love for God and one's neighbor. But religion is uncomfortable around simplicity. Instead of asking how God's Law should be kept, they asked, "How shall we not break it?" From that question, all manner of debates and questions arose that were finalized in the Pharisees' laws that were intended to keep a man from even coming close to breaking God's Law.

These man-made laws were called "fence laws," i.e., laws that fenced off God's Law, keeping the devout from even coming close to breaking it. They did not realize that, had they pursued love, they would have kept all of the Law and more. Instead, they dug themselves into the quagmire of endless, meaningless rules.

These fence laws covered every area of life. There were rules for how one dressed; what could be eaten and drunk; the places one could and could not go; what one could and, more importantly, what one could not do on the Sabbath day; the people one could not be associated with . . . plus hundreds of little rituals that had to be observed when one ate, prayed or fasted.

Even the secular Israelite was constantly reminded by them and felt regular twinges of guilt that he was not living up to the standard of holiness the Pharisees had declared as final truth.

The evil of the system was not in what the law prohibited and commanded (although most of it was a foolish exercise in futility), but in its *eros* root. The Pharisees' keeping of the rules was to be accepted by God; the level of their obedience to the Law was an indicator of where they stood on the ladder they laboriously climbed toward God. But however right the goal, God cannot be reached by the keeping of commands and the doing of rituals.

It was over against this form of religion that Jesus spoke His angriest words. When He saw what this belief system did to men, He was moved with compassion.

> **When He saw the throngs, He was moved with pity and sympathy for them, because they were bewildered — harassed and distressed and dejected and helpless — like sheep without a shepherd.**
>
> **Matthew 9:36 AMP**

To these sheep, weary and exhausted by the constant burdens laid on them by religion, Jesus said:

> **"Come to Me, all who are weary and heavy-laden, and I will give you rest.**
>
> **"Take My yoke upon you, and learn from Me, for I am gentle and humble in heart; and YOU SHALL FIND REST FOR YOUR SOULS.**
>
> **"For My yoke is easy, and My load is light."**
> **Matthew 11:28-30** NAS

The word, *weary* means, "worn out, to have worked until there is no strength left." Today, in the context in which Jesus was speaking, we could translate it as "spiritually burned out, depleted of all spiritual strength, exhausted in one's attempts to please God." These people were burdened, heavy laden with all the rules and formulas that religion had imposed upon them.

Jesus called them to come to Him and, in so doing, He threw down the gauntlet in the face of religion. He used the expression, **Take My yoke upon you . . .** (v. 29), the phrase that described the oath of allegiance to religion and all of its laws.

He was saying that He is the new *Torah*, the new Law that is not a list of commands, but a living Person, and to be yoked to Him gives rest. *The Amplified Bible* renders this verse: **. . . and you will find rest — relief, ease and refreshment and recreation and blessed quiet — for your souls.**

Religion brought spiritual burnout. Jesus promised that to come to Him would result in recreation, a vacation . . . . a life in which one would be continually refreshed and recreated in his relationship with Him.

Spiritual burnout can only occur where there is either a fundamental misunderstanding of the heart of the Gospel, or a failure to apply it to our lives and ministry. A spiritually exhausted believer is exhibiting symptoms of a much deeper problem.

25

---

[1]Noah Webster, *Webster's New 20th Century Dictionary of the English Language,* 2d ed. rev. (New York: Simon and Schuster, 1983).

Chapter 3

A NEW KIND OF LOVE

Jesus was the revelation of a kind of love about which the world, in their highest imagining, had never dreamed. The greatest minds of the world had sat and deliberated as to the nature of God or the gods. The highest thoughts they could achieve were an extension of the highest virtue they knew as fallen men — *eros*. Man can only know what God is like by the revelation He has made of Himself in Jesus.

It took another Greek word to describe this God-love, *agape*. The word was seldom used before Jesus came, and it took the writers of the New Testament, describing the revelation of God, to give definition to the word.

First John 4:8 (NAS) gives us its ultimate definition, **. . . God is love** *(agape)*. *Agape,* therefore, is not emotion that God has, but His very nature, the way He is. *Agape* is the eternal choice of God to be for others, to exist for the good of His creation. *Agape* draws no circles, excludes none.

Jesus spoke of the way God is in Matthew 5:44,45 (NAS):

". . . love your enemies, and pray for those who persecute you

in order that you may be sons of your Father who is in heaven; for He causes His sun to rise on the evil and the good, and sends rain on the righteous and the unrighteous."

And in Luke 6:35 (NAS):

"But love your enemies, and do good, and lend, expecting nothing in return . . . and you will be sons of the Most High; for He Himself is kind to ungrateful and evil men."

These two verses describe this God-love reaching out to all, down to His enemies, to the evil and the ungrateful, and not expecting any response. He loves because of Who He is, not because of any performance on the part of the loved. Men may walk away from Him, curse Him, and work to do things that grieve Him; but He continues to love them, willing and working for their highest good.

In Jesus, *agape* became flesh and lived and walked among us. In all that He was, said and did, we see the nature of this God-kind of love. In His death, *agape* finds its final definition. He died so that His enemies, those who hated Him, would not have to die!

The purest and only true religion in the world, the religion born at Mount Sinai through Moses, said, . . . **you shall love your neighbor as yourself** . . . (Lev. 19:18 NAS). Jesus didn't — He loved His neighbor more than Himself.

This kind of love cannot really be expressed in any language, so in the Old Testament God called one of His prophets, Hosea, to show *agape* through the events of his own life. In his capacity as the representative of God, Hosea's name was known in every household in Israel. He and his family were watched by all.

God called Hosea to marry Gomer, a woman with unfaithfulness in her heart. It wasn't long into the marriage before her unfaithfulness began to make itself manifest. She was seen with different men at the parties of the "jet set" of Samaria, and all the nation of Israel began to watch the soap opera unfolding before their eyes.

Finally, she left Hosea and became a prostitute. In the eyes of decent people, she was a slut who was making a fool out of her husband. All her actions made it plain that she despised Hosea and wanted to embarrass him before the watching Israel.

Then, her many lovers tired of her. She found herself having to sell her body on the streets, the slave of a pimp. He finally put her on the slave stand, for sale to the highest bidder.

Hosea has been deeply hurt . . . he is lonely and his tears have flowed freely from the burning shame of the public scandal. And now with his wife for sale on the slave stand, he is told by God to go and purchase her and reinstate her as his wife: "Love the woman who has shamed and despised you, seek her highest good, bring her to your house, protect and care for her."

As Hosea made his way through the back streets of Samaria to the slave market, each step was etching into the minds of Israel the nature of the love God has for us.

Eros rejects the ugly and those that hurt it; *agape* reaches out to its enemies and seeks their highest good. *Eros* says, "I love you because I need you!" *Agape* says, "I need you because I love you!"

Hosea's unceasing love for his wife became God's message to Israel, a shadowy picture of His love to mankind. It is this same incredible love that caused Jesus to weep audibly over Jerusalem (Luke 19:41-44), not because they were going to insult, shame and crucify Him; but because in so doing, they were eternally hurting themselves. He wept for the hurt of His enemies.

Jesus, *Agape*, died for us and rose from the dead — and He gives to all men who will receive it, the gift of His eternal life. The only response man can make to God's gift of *agape* is faith in Who He is and what He has done. Even that faith, by which a man receives that love into his life to make him whole, is the gift of God.

When Jesus sat and ate with the immoral scum of Galilee, a new word was being birthed into the human vocabulary, *grace*. It had been used in Old Testament times, but it received its fullest and clearest definition in Jesus.

Grace is a rich word in the Greek language. It was used on the streets of Greece and Rome long before the Holy Spirit adopted it into the New Testament. The Greek word for grace is *charis.*

It had the meaning of "something that delights or brings joy, a favor, something given that is not earned." The word might be used to describe a birthday present or something one would do for a neighbor or friend.

Charis is perfectly expressed in a custom of the Roman emperors. Each year, a day was set aside to celebrate the ascension of the emperor to the throne. On that day he gave, from his own purse, a bonus to his soldiers. This had nothing to do with the wages they earned; this was the emperor's gift and was called, "the *charis*." The soldiers did not work for it, it came out of the generosity of the emperor's heart.

When the Greeks greeted one another, they used the word *charis*. They began all of their letters with the same word. It was a wish, a desire that the other person's life would be filled with good things, favors from the gods that would fill the life with beauty and joy. Similarly, when wine glasses touched in bars and at weddings, the toast was, "*Charis* to you!"

Expressing the heart of God in His giving us salvation in Jesus, it was a perfect word to be incorporated into the vocabulary of the Gospel.

However, the word needed to have its meaning expanded to describe the news of how God gives to us.

The definition was enlarged to include the idea of not only an unearned favor, but a favor that was not deserved, a gift that was, in fact, the reverse of what was deserved. We do not deserve God's gifts and there is nothing we could do to earn them, but God gives them — that is grace.

Charis, when used as a greeting or toast, was a pleasantry that had no power to implement its wishes. When brought into the Christian vocabulary, it was endowed with the power of God.

God does not wish us well; rather, He effectually works His salvation in our lives.

His Gospel is the power of God to salvation. (Rom. 1:16.) The early Christians continued the Greek custom of opening their letters with the *charis* greeting, but added the authority and power of **. . . from God our Father and the Lord Jesus Christ** (2 Cor. 1:2 NAS).

The New Testament believers never thought of *charis* as being a quality locked up in the heart of God. The word is always linked to the coming of Jesus, His death and resurrection — the events which actualized the grace of God in human history. Its power is seen released in the proclamation of the Gospel.

The Gospel is the call to rest, to receive the free, undeserved gift that God has given us in Christ. There is nothing man can do to earn salvation from his past, or his present acceptance and walk with God. It is, from beginning to end, the *charis* of God, which can only be received by faith.

God is not for sale! The ladders man erects and the man-made rules he keeps while seeking to ascend to God — all are an insult to the *Agape* God Who freely gives Himself to all.

The spirit of religion rages against the God Who freely loves and gives Himself for all. *Eros* hates *agape!* The mind of the flesh insists that man earn his acceptance with God. Even if he must receive his pardon freely from God, the natural man believes he must now work in order to be worthy to receive continuing favor from Him.

The body of truth that proclaims the revelation of God is called the Good News. News, by definition, is the announcement of something that has *happened,* not a list of things that must be done! All that must be done for a man to live in perfect union with God has been accomplished by Jesus in His death and resurrection.

There is nothing left for man to do, no ladders to climb, no mountains to scale. The heart of the Christian life is to stand in wonder before His love and say, "Thank You!"

When we begin to add conditions to God's gift, for whatever reason, our descent into Pharisaism and spiritual burnout has begun. The death that has crept into the pot to feed the spirits of multitudes today is the poisonous weed of a belief system that calls man to keep religious rules in order to continue being accepted by God.

Many of the stories that Jesus told were in response to the spirit the Pharisees expressed when they saw the kind of people He accepted. These stories illustrate the wonder of *agape* and *charis* that stream to us from God.

One day, Jesus was eating with some of the most immoral people — the tax collectors, and other assorted persons. The Pharisees despised these people whom they dismissed as "sinners."

In Bible days the act of eating was more than having a meal to satisfy hunger, it was a commitment to lasting friendship . . . a promise to be there when the other person needed you. With disgust, the Pharisees grumbled as they watched; Jesus was the scandal of religion!

He called them over and began telling stories to His dinner guests and, also, to these proud Pharisees.

He told of a father who had two sons. Apparently, both sons chafed under the discipline that went with the running of the farm. They looked upon their father as a slave driver, rather than as the senior partner in a farm that would soon be theirs. Their negative attitude blinded both of them to the true heart of the man — a heart of love and kindness to all.

The younger son came to his father and asked for the share of the inheritance that was to be his. The language Jesus puts in the young man's mouth is legal terminology — either the boy had a lawyer or he had consulted one.

Legally, his share would not come to him until his father died, a provision that guaranteed the father would be looked after while he lived. What the young man was really saying was, "I can't wait until you die, give me the cash now!" Words that would cut deep into any parent's heart.

The law of inheritance gave the oldest son two-thirds of the inheritance; the younger, one-third. The father does not fight the request. He gives the boy his third, and *he* immediately sets off for a far country.

The expression, "far country," in the ears of an Israelite, meant a place away from the covenant people, among the Gentiles. Gentiles were despised and hated by the Pharisees, and they would already judge the boy as beyond hope.

In the far country, the cash was quickly spent in wild living. By the time he ran out of cash, a famine had come to the land. Destitute and starving, the man went to work for a farmer as a pig herder. To the Jew, this was as low as a man could get. The Levitical Law described the pig as an unclean and detestable animal. To eat or touch it was to share its uncleanness and become as detestable as it was. A person who touched pigs was no longer welcome among the covenant people.

One day, as he looked at his rags and the filth in which he lived, he remembered something about his father. It didn't seem like very much, but he remembered that his dad looked after his hired servants well. They always had enough on which to live . . . and always had some left over. He made up his mind to go and ask his father to be considered as a hired servant.

He rehearsed what he was going to say. He simply stated that he had sinned against God and his father, and asked to be a hired servant. A hired servant was not on the payroll, did not live with the servants on the farm and had no contact with the family. He was hired by the day whenever there was need for extra help.

He made no promises, asked for no second chance at being a son . . . he simply responded to the remembrance of his dad's kindness and care for the hired help.

Meanwhile, neither of the boys understood that their father had never stopped loving this son who was lost among the Gentiles.

As the father had given him the money, he had forgiven the son for his selfish, callous words. Through all of the time he had been away, even through rumors of what his son was doing, there was no resentment or bitterness. His love for the boy was bigger than all the boy had done to him; he hurt for how the boy must be feeling, wherever he was, and only wanted him home.

Watching for him, the father scanned the horizon daily. And the moment he came over the horizon, the father saw him. He didn't wait for the boy to get to the house, but ran to where he was, flung his arms around the emaciated body that reeked of pigs.

The father smothered him with kisses and refused to allow the boy to ask to become a hired servant. Instead, he robed him with his own best robe, put shoes on his feet and his own ring on the boy's finger! He then led him back to the house for a meal to celebrate his reinstatement as a son in the family.

At this point in the story, the Pharisees would have shown utter disgust. In their opinion, such a worthless son, who had left the covenant people, was fit only for hell. If they happened to touch a man who had pig muck on his clothes, they would immediately go and bathe and wash their clothes. To embrace such a person and get some of that filth on their own person was too revolting for words . . . and to kiss a pig herder would be like having a love affair with a loathsome toad!

The point Jesus was making was obvious. He was saying that God was not at all like they imagined Him to be. God loves the worst of people, people whose lives are hopelessly messed up. He doesn't hold their sins against them; but rather, He embraces people who smell of pigs, He pardons and smothers them with His kisses.

Chapter 4

SLAVES VERSUS SONS

At this point in the story, Jesus introduced the character of the elder brother in order to show, by vivid contrast, the true nature of the Pharisee belief system. The brother is seen to be bankrupt of the love that is seen in his father but, also, totally ignorant of it and is its sworn enemy.

He had been working in the fields all day. As he returned, he heard the sound of loud music and dancing. Annoyed, he asked a servant, who was hurrying by, what was happening.

Excitedly, the servant told him that his brother had returned and the party was his welcome home celebration. His eyes became dark with rage . . . he turned back to the fields, refusing to go inside. His brother disgusted him; he despised his memory and, inwardly, raged against his father.

Hearing that he was not willing to welcome his brother, the father came out to plead with him to come inside. Sullenly, he refused and, then, exploded at his father.

" '. . . Look! For so many years I have been serving you, and I have never neglected a command of yours; and yet you have never given me a kid, that I might be merry with my friends;

but when this son of yours came, who has devoured your wealth with harlots, you killed the fattened calf for him.' "

Luke 15:29,30 NAS

In his anger, he showed the nature of his heart all through the years. He said, "I have been serving you, and I have never neglected a command of yours." The Greek word for *serve* is "to slave." *The New English Bible* translates it as, **. . . I have slaved for you all these years . . .** (v. 29). He had chafed under what he had perceived as rules laid down by his slave-driving father. He saw himself as a slave, quick to do all he was commanded.

Because of this perverted idea, he perceived his father's words through the ears of a slave. When the father said to him, "The fences need fixing," he was speaking to his son and co-owner of the farm. He was really saying, "It would be a wise investment in our property if we fixed the fences today." As heard through the ears of the elder brother, it translated, "Fix the fences, boy!"

As a slave, in his opinion, he was doing well. He had always done as he was told — even though he didn't always enjoy or agree with it. But he had never begun to understand the idea of a love relationship in which, as a son, he knew that he was accepted and loved for who he was and as he was.

Nor did he know the joy of loving his father or brother with that kind of love. There had never been a day when he had worked for the sheer love of his father, to provide for him and, at the same time, thrill to being the co-owner of the farm with him.

Now the younger brother, who has flagrantly disobeyed and shamed his father, has come home. And father gives him a party!

There were no words to express the older brother's feelings of rejection. He felt his father was grossly unfair. What he couldn't see was that, anytime, he could have thrown a party (even one for his dad, if he had wanted) for he was co-owner of the farm.

The fact is, the mentality of a slave does not breed parties and spontaneous celebrations of joy. It breeds fear and the cowering question, "I never seem to please him — have I done enough yet?"

He probably had never wanted a party — until he saw his brother in the midst of such gaiety.

He raged, "It isn't fair, he hasn't done what I have! He hasn't slaved and obeyed your every command as I have. When will I do enough to please you?"

What he and the Pharisees whom he represented were blind to was the fact that acceptance had nothing to do with actions or behavior. It had everything to do with the father's love; and on the part of the younger brother, faith in that incredible love.

The Pharisee believed that his diary of accomplishments would earn him favor with God. In approaching God, he held up his time sheet to the One he perceived as the tyrant slave owner. He recited his accomplishments and bemoaned his failures, whining to Him how prone he was to fail.

The Pharisees would have been stunned by Jesus' story. The father had bypassed the elder son's behavior and, in so doing, was saying that it had nothing to do with acceptance or rejection. Acceptance depended on who the father was, not on what the son had done.

In that it subtracts from a person's lifestyle many things he has been doing and adds many other things that have never been part of his life, religion is behavior modification. Its emphasis is on externals: the clothes one may not wear; the places that must be avoided; the books, magazines, movies that are taboo; the food and drink that must not be touched.

It also adds new behavior: total involvement in church or religious meetings, disciplined times for Bible reading and prayer, social work among the poor. Friends change to include only those who share the same religious lifestyle and who, together, are involved in all the social activities that are acceptable within the code of that particular expression of religion. One may be more devoted to God by becoming a deacon, choir member, youth leader, minister or, even, a missionary!

It is obvious that the belief system of the Pharisee, seeking acceptance with God by changing one's behavior, reduces Christianity to a formula instead of the dynamic relationship with God that Jesus came to bring.

When the elder son referred to him as, "this son of yours," rather than as his brother, he was indicating that he felt the younger brother's behavior had forfeited him his place in the family.

But it's worse than this, for living by rules and codes inevitably produces the reverse of the goals of Jesus. God is *agape,* and Jesus said that His followers would be known by a lifestyle of the God-kind of love. Tragically, religion can only produce pride in a person's heart and a despising of all those who do not follow its particular rules.

The elder brother despised this younger brother because of his behavior. In his own mind he had, when referring to him as "this son of yours" rather than his brother, cut him out of the family without mercy or forgiveness. Religion, looking at itself in the mirror of its commandments and then out to those who do not belong to the same persuasion, preens itself, " '. . . **God, I thank Thee that I am not like other people . . .'** " (Luke 18:11 NAS). Then it goes on to describe to himself his own superior lifestyle!

Throughout history the Spirit of God has continually broken in among men and opened their eyes to see His incredible, unconditional love to them in Christ.

When man receives the gift of *agape,* there is joy and celebration. But within a short time, like weeds in a flower bed, Pharisee leaders appear who reduce the spontaneous life of the Spirit to a rigid code. Their relationship with God has been reduced to a dead formula for living.

The believer is no longer known by Christ being the source of his life, but by the peculiarities of the rules he lives by. Witnessing ceases to be a sharing of Jesus himself; it becomes an invitation to come under the yoke of a particular brand of religion.

The more religious a person becomes, the further away from God he grows. With increased dedication comes an increased sense of emptiness. Keeping all the rules does not satisfy the hunger within; and so, dedication follows dedication, always with the hope that this will be the ultimate offering that will please God and bring the heart to satisfaction.

There is also agonizing frustration! The heart does not want to keep the rules; there is a desire to break out, which only brings constant confession of failure when approaching God.

We once had a dog named Fred. Fred was a cheerful little creature, but had the annoying habit of playfully biting the legs of anyone who walked down our drive, especially the mailman. If we were to keep the dog, something had to be done — and so we muzzled him.

To the relief of the mailman, Fred now sat with a muzzle over his mouth. People could now walk our path in safety. However, although he was now a safe dog, nothing had changed in Fred. Everyday, he sat lusting after all the legs that went past. We had changed his behavior, but not his disposition!

Religion changes behavior but not the heart, the source of man's "want to's." Following all of the rules, the believer avoids what is forbidden . . . but his heart still wants to do it. In fact, the heart now wants to do it more than before it was forbidden. The sincere person becomes disgusted with his inability to obey, and returns to dedications and promises to God.

It is this sincere person who, sooner or later, is going to be in trouble, burned out and spiritually exhausted. Some people can live with the difference between the rules and the way things really are; but the candidate for spiritual burnout cannot live with what he rightly sees as hypocrisy.

As he continues to struggle for spiritual maturity within the framework of the codes of his church, he becomes confused, disheartened and soured. His enthusiasm wanes, and he realizes that he is only going through the motions. Finally, he drops from the scene, burned out by the teaching he has received.

The only real enemy a believer has is the slave mentality that constantly struggles to win God's favor. All of God's blessing belong to him until he seeks to earn them by behavior modification. While checking on his actions to see if he is acceptable to God, he falls helplessly into the hands of the devil, the accuser of the brethren.

Jesus exposed the spirit of Pharisaism as antagonistic to His Father's heart and the Gospel. He warned his disciples, **. . . "Watch out! Beware of the leaven of the Pharisees . . ."** (Mark 8:15 NAS). He could see that the deadly doctrine would penetrate among even those who had been with Him and had seen His holy rage against it.

Reading the account of the Holy Spirit coming at Pentecost, we forget the fact that those first believers were locked into the religious culture of their birth. They had received the Spirit, but their minds thought of walking with God and holiness in the way they had been raised, which, to some degree or another, was Pharisaism.

Steeped in the teaching they had received from the rabbis since they were children, and having a respect for the Pharisee as the holiest of all men, it was unthinkable to them that anyone could truly know God until he had submitted to the yoke of the Law.

They did not heed the warning of Jesus, even if they understood what He meant. Under the leadership of James, for the first decades after Pentecost, the Church in Jerusalem saw Jesus as the Messiah exclusively for the Jews. They believed He had come to bring about a kingdom in which everyone perfectly kept the letter of the Law.

Many Pharisees came to know Jesus after Pentecost. However, when they accepted Him, they did not cease to live by the commands of the Law. They assumed that, because they knew Christ, He would help them keep all the rituals and formulas of the Old Testament Law — as well as their man-made fence laws.

They felt it was their duty to teach all outsiders who came to Christ how to live by the rules. The Pharisees saw themselves as having entered the kingdom already educated, and so now they could help these poor, ignorant Gentiles to be as spiritual as they were. It never occurred to them that Christ's death and resurrection had brought an end to religion and the beginning of a new method of living.

Paul and Barnabas went to the Gentiles, first to Antioch in Syria and then to Asia Minor, announcing that all may approach God through what Christ had done — without first bringing their behavior in line with God's Law. Antioch became a center of joyous celebration in God's *agape* and grace.

The tension, between what the Church in Jerusalem under the leadership of James was saying and what Paul was preaching, became tense. It was decided to have a conference in which the issue could be discussed openly with the guidance of the Holy Spirit.

At the conference the Spirit opened the eyes of the Jerusalem believers, including James, and they saw that His grace and love was for everyone . . . without having to earn it by keeping the Law of Moses or the laws of the Pharisees. The company returned to Antioch, rejoicing that the Spirit had prevailed and saved the Church from the slave mentality of the elder brother.

Peter came and spent time with the disciples in Antioch, and lived freely among them without observing any of the Pharisees' rules. One day, some men came from the church in Jerusalem. Immediately, Peter began acting like a Pharisee and the Jewish people in the church followed his lead. Even Barnabas gave in and began keeping fence laws.

Paul realized that this was no local squabble over how a believer should live. He saw that the Gospel was at stake: either a person is accepted by God based on his attempts to keep God's Law and the man-made rules of a church group, or he is accepted based on God's free love and grace. There can be no middle ground.

He rose and confronted Peter before the whole group. His final word to Peter shows the eternal seriousness of the issue: **"I do not nullify the grace of God; for if righteousness comes through the Law, then Christ died needlessly"** (Gal. 2:21 NAS).

If a person seeks acceptance with God based in any way upon the way he has ordered his life, he is stating that the death of Christ was unnecessary. Paul could not have said it plainer than he did that day in Antioch.

But the spirit of religion is persistent. Paul and Barnabas had preached the Gospel of God's grace throughout Galatia; thousands had accepted Christ and begun to live in the power of Christ within them.

The Jews, who accepted Christ, no longer lived by Pharisee laws, but lived by the Spirit within. Gentiles, who had come from an immoral, idolatrous society, were learning to walk in love from Him who lived within, with no reference to rules and prohibitions.

Then came some of the believing Pharisees from Jerusalem. Apparently, they had privately disagreed with the conclusions of the conference (it is questionable as to whether James really understood what the Spirit had revealed at the conference).

They congratulated the Galatians on accepting Christ and then asked, "And how do you now plan to order your lives to please God?" They went on to rebuke the Jews for abandoning the Law, assuring them that now they had the power to keep every command and, only as they did so, would God be pleased. They put pressure on the Gentiles to come under the yoke of the Law, so that they would not return to the lawless and immoral society from which they had so recently come.

Their argument makes sense to the natural mind:

"Surely, it is necessary to lay down regulations and directions: let us have steps we can climb toward the goal of spiritual maturity.

"In an idolatrous and immoral society like Galatia, we need to have rules that govern how we dress, what we eat and drink, how many hours we should spend in prayer and meditation and how often each week we should attend the gathering of the believers.

"We need guidelines like these so we can be a good witness. They will know we are Christians by our dress, our abstentions and our church attendance. We need rules within the Church to judge who is spiritual and who is worldly."

All of this makes so much sense to the flesh, but it is antagonistic to God!

When Paul heard what the Pharisee party had done among his Galatian converts, he wrote them a letter. Again, his words could not be plainer; this was not some nonessential doctrine where believers could have legitimate disagreement.

> **I am amazed that you are so quickly deserting Him who called you by the grace of Christ, for a different gospel;**
>
> **which is really not another; only there are some who are disturbing you, and want to distort the gospel of Christ.**
>
> **But even though we, or an angel from heaven, should preach to you a gospel contrary to that which we have preached to you, let him be accursed.**
>
> **As we have said before, so I say again now, if any man is preaching to you a gospel contrary to that which you received, let him be accursed.**
>
> **Galatians 1:6-9 NAS**

These are among the strongest words in the New Testament. They show us that to believe that we need to change our behavior in order to enjoy God's favor is to do away with the work of Christ!

"May God damn any man who teaches this," said Paul. Yet, it is the poison that is in the pot from which so many believers are eating today. It is this ingredient that is turning sons of God into whimpering slaves, struggling to obey commands. It is this leaven of the Pharisees that has caused the epidemic of burned-out believers, who lie exhausted by the roadside of life.

Do you remember the day you first saw the grace of God? You rejoiced in Jesus and what He had done, Who He was in your life . . . for days! A spontaneous love for everyone sprang up in your heart; a childlike delight in life gave you such an aura of joy that even cynical friends had to comment.

You were amazed at the way some of the old habits dropped off and a new lifestyle began to emerge from within. It was as if prison doors had opened, and you walked out as free as a bird.

Above everything else, you had an insatiable hunger for God. You lived in the consciousness of His presence all of the time, knowing what Paul meant when he said that we were to pray without ceasing. You wanted to know His Truth, and so you read the Scriptures avidly.

It's at this time in their Christian life that many are side-tracked by a believing Pharisee. It may be the pastor of a fellowship, a radio or television evangelist or a member of a prayer group or Bible study who has been a Christian for some time.

The reasoning is that, if the person is filled with the Spirit, then everything he says must be right. Therefore, the message of becoming a mature believer by obedience to the rules and formulas is accepted.

The message makes sense to the flesh. Freedom in Christ is relinquished for the bondage of Pharisaism. Under the yoke of bondage, the spontaneous life of Christ within becomes a memory and the joy of the Lord disappears.

It's only a matter of time before such a person, either inside or outside of the Church, becomes burned out, spiritually exhausted.

Chapter 5

FALSE SHEPHERDS

There are thousands of burned out and confused people who have left the Church because a sincere shepherd fed them from the poisoned pot of pharisaical legalism.

Jesus often used the imagery of shepherd and sheep to describe the reason He came to earth. This was not original to Jesus. In fact, it is a picture that God often used to describe His relationship to His covenant people. It was Jacob who was the first to speak of Him in this way (Gen. 48:15; 49:24), and David immortalized the picture in Psalm 23.

In Bible days, a shepherd meant a lot more than it does today. The shepherd gave himself to his flock; he was totally responsible for their protection and sustenance. When the term was used symbolically, it described the leaders, both the king and the spiritual leaders, of a nation. All were seen as responsible for the care, food and guidance of the people in their particular areas.

But it was in the prophets that the imagery was really developed. The burden of more than one prophet was to point out that God's covenant people had been led astray by false shepherds.

What had the shepherds taught the people that caused them to be scattered and left prey to every enemy that sought to kill them? The prophet Zechariah spoke to it:

. . . Therefore the people wander like sheep,

They are afflicted because there is no shepherd.

Zechariah 10:2 NAS

". . . a shepherd . . . who will not care for the perishing, seek the scattered, heal the broken, or sustain the one standing, but will devour the flesh of the fat sheep . . ."

Zechariah 11:16 NAS

Ezekiel 34:4-8 spoke of it clearer than any other prophet:

"Those who are sickly you have not strengthened, the diseased you have not healed, the broken you have not bound up, the scattered you have not brought back, nor have you sought for the lost; but with force and with severity you have dominated them.

"And they were scattered for lack of a shepherd, and they became food for every beast of the field . . .

"My flock wandered through all the mountains . . . no one to search or seek for them . . .

". . . My flock has become a prey, My flock has even become food for all the beasts of the field for lack of a shepherd, and My shepherds did not search for My flock . . ."

Ezekiel 34:4-8 NAS

As God saw His sheep harassed and hurt by the shepherds who held the position that was intended to guarantee their health, protection and guidance, He said that He himself would come and be their Shepherd.

For thus saith the Lord God,

"Behold, I Myself will search for My sheep and seek them out.

"As a shepherd cares for his herd in the day when he is among his scattered sheep, so I will care for My sheep and deliver them

**from all the places to which they were scattered on a cloudy and
gloomy day . . .**

**"I will feed My flock and I will lead them to rest," declares the
Lord God.**

**"I will seek the lost, bring back the scattered, bind up the broken,
and strengthen the sick . . ."**

Ezekiel 34:11,15,16 NAS

Jesus spoke of Himself as the covenant Shepherd-God who
had come to gather together His sheep, heal them and bring them
to rest and safety. He used the language of Ezekiel to describe His
mission. **"For the Son of Man has come to seek and to save that which
was lost"** (Luke 19:10 NAS).

He saw the people as the broken sheep of whom the prophets
had spoken: **. . . He felt compassion for them because they were like
sheep without a shepherd . . .** (Mark 6:34 NAS). **And seeing the
multitudes, He felt compassion for them, because they were distressed
and downcast like sheep without a shepherd** (Matt. 9:36 NAS).

There are two vivid words used here to describe the condition
of the sheep. The word translated as **distressed** has been used in
the Greek language to describe a person who has been attacked,
his valuables stolen. He now lies frightened, bewildered, too weak
to move from the side of the road where he has been left. **Downcast,**
the second word, has also been used to describe a person who has
fallen down and is helpless to get up.

To look at the crowd of people, one would have seen a group
of decent, respectable peasants from Galilee, who attended worship
every Sabbath and sent their children to a school where the main
textbook was the first five books of the Bible. Most of the families
read and memorized much of the Scriptures, and their lives were
ordered around trying to obey their precepts.

Jesus saw them with the eyes of the covenant Shepherd. He
described these fine people as lost, beaten sheep who, having had
the truth stolen from them, were bewildered and ready to give up.
Their spiritual leaders had so distorted the truth of God's Word

47

that it had become a source of death and spiritual exhaustion to them.

When we say that Jesus seeks the lost, we think of Him seeking all sinners, whoever and wherever they are, and for whatever reason they are lost. This is true.

But originally, Jesus was describing His coming to seek those who had been confused and beaten with words by those who were the alleged shepherds. The lost were the common people who sat in the synagogue every Sabbath, wondering if they could ever be good enough for God to love. The lost were also those who, if they ever thought of approaching God, were driven away by the spiritual leaders.

The Pharisees were the most vocal in their denunciation of tax collectors, prostitutes, thieves and other assorted sinners from the back alleys of Jerusalem. From their pulpits, they announced that God delighted to damn in hell these vermin because of their behavior. The Pharisees were scandalized by Jesus who made these folk, these "sinners," His friends and disciples.

Today, Jesus still seeks sheep who are lost because they have been beaten to exhaustion by the words of those who speak in His Name.

Many people in the United States have been to a Sunday school of some church, and a great number have been to a church school. Yet, they have fled from what they heard! Why? Was it because they were God haters? No!

They fled because a shepherd, speaking as the representative of God, presented a Gospel that was corrupt with the leaven of the Pharisees. He demanded they change their behavior to conform to a lifestyle that would earn them God's favor.

Fifteen years ago, I was the speaker at a teenage camp in the Northwest. The camp was sponsored by a group of evangelical churches who also believed that Christians should have the experience of being filled with the Spirit. All of the teens came from Christian homes. Their parents were members of the churches; many were active as deacons, elders and choir leaders. Some of the group were from the homes of pastors.

The pastors, who were in charge of the camp, met with me before the meetings and shared that all of the sponsoring churches were concerned with the spiritual state of their teens. Apparently, as they entered their teenage years, they had become disinterested in the things of God, and some had openly rebelled against their parents and the church.

The first meetings were difficult. About 150 teens sat or, rather, sprawled in their seats. Many had glazed eyes; others blew large pink bubbles with their gum or yawned interminably.

The third night, I sat on the edge of the stage and asked for their help in getting to understand what they believed. There was a flicker of interest which I knew arose from the fact that, tonight, there would not be a sermon!

Assuring them I would not criticize, I encouraged them to answer my questions. I started with, "What is a Christian?"

After a brief silence, a girl of about 14 raised her hand and said, "You have to accept Jesus as your Savior."

I nodded and asked, "How do you do that?"

Another hand went up, "You put up your hand in a meeting and walk forward and pray."

"Why do you do that?" I asked. "What do you pray for when you walk forward?"

More hands went up, and I selected a freckle-faced youth two rows from the front.

"You promise God you are going to be better . . . give up sin," he volunteered. Another shouted, "You ask Him to help you to be good!"

"Okay," I asked, "what happens if you become a Christian?"

A ripple of whispers and snickers went through the crowd. Finally, one girl put up her hand. "It's worse for a girl!" she said hesitantly, and then blushed and giggled.

I was surprised at the answer and encouraged her to explain what she meant. "Well, Christian girls can't wear mini-skirts or makeup . . ." and again she blushed into silence. Other girls loudly agreed and added, "We can't get our hair permed or wear ear rings."

Convinced now there was not going to be a sermon, they were visibly waking up. The boys began to join in, volunteering their lists of things Christians couldn't do. Smoking cigarettes headed the list, followed by drinking beer and wine, swearing, listening to rock music and reading *Playboy*.

As their answers came, I glanced over at the pastors. I was amazed to see that, smiling and nodding their heads, they were approving, agreeing with what the teens were saying.

I pointed out that they had only told me what Christians cannot do and asked, "How do Christians spend their time?"

There was silence, then a voice from the middle of the crowd shouted, "They don't do much!" This was greeted with laughter, and someone else shouted, "They go bowling on Monday with their parents to watch them!" This was accompanied with hoots and more laughter.

There was a long silence, and then answers began to trickle in with little enthusiasm. Going to church all day on Sunday and on Wednesday night was, they all agreed, an absolute must. Others suggested reading the Bible and praying for half an hour every morning.

It became apparent that the really dedicated Christians were those who witnessed to people in the shopping malls on Saturday, left tracts for waitresses in restaurants (sometimes instead of tips) and went from door to door, inviting people to church.

"What motivates Christians to do all these things?" I asked. Again, silence.

The serious girl in the front row said, "You have to try very hard, pray a lot, dedicate your life to Jesus all the time and listen to Christian radio."

"Does anyone really live like this?" I asked.

They looked at each other and there was a lot of fidgeting. "Most backslide a lot," said a boy beside the solemn girl.

When I asked, "What do you do then?" One answered, "Walk forward, rededicate your life and try again!"

I waited in a silence that was almost friendly and then said, "Do you think that being a Christian is the most fantastic life on earth?" They were not expecting such a question, and burst into peals of laughter. Finally, one gasped, "You've got to be crazy!"

I was amazed that these teenagers who had been exposed to so many meetings, so many speakers, as well as their own pastor week after week, had missed the Gospel entirely. How could their parents, some of them I knew as Spirit-filled believers, have given this impression?

"Where does Jesus fit into all this?" I asked when the laughter had subsided. There was an immediate clamor of hands. They all agreed that He had died for them.

"Well, what do you mean by that?" I pressed my question in the light of such enthusiasm. Again the answer came quickly, "He died for our sins so that we could go to heaven."

"Are you sure you're going to heaven?" I asked casually to no one in particular.

"Only if you try hard to please God . . ." It was the solemn girl on the front row who addressed me with her counsel. I was going to ask how I could please God, but I knew we would be back to walking forward and dedicating, so I let it pass.

"Okay, what does it mean then that Jesus rose from the dead?"

There was a long silence, and it got a little uncomfortable. Finally, someone said that it meant that He was with people every day, helping them to be good, dedicated Christians.

I asked if it meant that He would help them not to wear miniskirts or drink wine, and to read the Bible instead of *Playboy* every day. Everyone looked uncomfortable, and some nodded sheepishly. I knew I was into areas they obviously hadn't thought about.

I backed off, and let them ask me general questions about the Bible. I had enough insight to where they stood to give me direction in my preaching for the next week.

Afterward, I talked with the ministers who led the camp. One said, "Well, now you have seen for yourself! These teens know what holiness is, but they don't want to pay the price!" I was stunned; momentarily, I felt I was sitting in old Jerusalem talking with James or one of his believing pharisaical assistants!

The believers in the churches that sponsored the camp are like many thousands of believers throughout the English-speaking world. They were all truly born again and filled with the Spirit.

At some point, years before, Jesus had so filled and enthused their lives that many of the components of their old lifestyle fell away and were replaced with a life that expressed Jesus. God's grace had come to them, and His love had expelled their old life patterns.

But it wasn't long before they forgot that God had loved them while they had been living the old lifestyle. He had loved them while they were drunk, and as they had whirled around the dance floor. They so completely forgot it that they began to equate their present life in the grace of God with their giving up of their old life — as if they had earned their place in God by giving up the old ways.

No one would remember the day they made an appendix to the Gospel. It became a rule in the church that anyone, who was really serious with God, had to give up the things the original membership had given up and adopt their lifestyle. What had been grace to them in the beginning, had now become law to their children. And through their rules, they were now driving their children away from Jesus.

And they were so sincere! They really believed that they were keeping their children from sin, not realizing that, in actual fact, they were making sin very alluring to them. Nor did they realize that the very existence of their rules denied that only Jesus, by His death and resurrection, could deliver and keep from sin.

Last year, I spoke to one of the pastors who had been a leader at that camp. "Do you remember that camp fifteen years ago?" I asked. "Whatever happened to those teenagers?"

Sadly, he shook his head. "They were rebellious and almost all of them went into the world."

No, they were not rebellious. They did not run away from Jesus — they had never met Him. They had fled, weary and exhausted, from religion that portrayed a mean, angry God who only loved people the Church deemed good.

Chapter 6

*THE **ZOE** LIFE*

In John 10, Jesus described the false shepherds as thieves, robbers and murderers. At best, they were hired servants, working only for wages, those who had no concern for the welfare of the sheep. At worst, they were likened to thieves stealing into the sheepfold to steal from their hearers all that the Father had freely given in His love.

They were murderers who brought spiritual death with their words. **"The thief comes only to steal, and kill, and destroy; . . . a hireling . . . is not concerned about the sheep"** (John 10:10,13 NAS).

Many have suggested that the thief is the devil, but the context does not allow that interpretation. The thief in this passage is the person who is teaching the sheep a doctrine that destroys their spiritual lives. In the context of John 10, that was the Pharisees.

Jesus has nothing in common with religion, any more than the shepherd has anything in common with the poacher. He did not come to give us strength to keep the Ten Commandments, nor did He give us an updated version of them in the Sermon on the Mount.

He gave no fence laws. In fact, He dismissed the fence laws of His day with scathing words. He himself blatantly violated them and encouraged His followers to do the same.

Jesus was opposed to any system that told man to change his behavior in order to be acceptable to God. He did not come to found a new religion. The Church He died and rose again to bring into existence is not a religion at all.

He describes Himself and His mission:

". . . I came that they might have life, and might have it abundantly.

"I am the good shepherd; the good shepherd lays down His life for the sheep."

John 10:10,11 NAS

We will feel the force of what He is saying here by understanding the meaning of the word He uses for life. In the Greek language, the word is *zoe. Zoe* is defined as, ". . . life in the absolute sense, life as God has it, that which the Father has in Himself, and which He gave to the Incarnate Son to have in Himself . . ."[1]

Zoe is the life that was expressed in the Word which spoke creation into being and is the foundation of all life in the universe. It is the life of God and is, therefore, not understood merely as an extension of days and activities, but as a quality and intensity of life.

. . . God is love . . . *(agape)* (1 John 4:16 NAS), and so His life, the way He is, is *agape*. The *zoe* of God came to live among us in Jesus. He said of Himself, **"I am the life . . ."** *(zoe)* (John 14:6 NAS). When John looked back to the the years he spent with Jesus in His earthly life, he exclaimed:

What was from the beginning, what we have heard, what we have seen with our eyes, what we beheld and our hands handled, concerning the Word of Life *(zoe)* —

and the life *(zoe)* **was manifested, and we have seen and bear witness and proclaim to you the eternal life** *(zoe)***, which was with the Father and was manifested to us —**

1 John 1:1,2 NAS

The final definition of *zoe* is "the life of Jesus"; it is life as Jesus lived it.

In his original creation, man partook of God's life and nature. **Then the Lord God formed man of dust from the ground, and breathed into his nostrils the breath of life . . .** (Gen. 2:7 NAS).

In the midst of his paradise home was the Tree of Life, of which he was allowed to eat. But in the Fall, he was cut off from this life. **. . . being darkened in their understanding, excluded from the life** *(zoe)* **of God . . .** (Eph. 4:18 NAS).

From that time forward, man is described as being dead. Certainly, he is alive in his mind and body and, along with all created life, he is upheld by *zoe*. But man did not know the Person Who is *zoe*; and since knowing Him was the reason of his creation, that means man is dead.

Man now had an extension of days in which he lived out his relationships, dreamed his dreams, set his goals, acquired his wealth and won his battles. But there was a vacuum at his center that was made to be filled with the *zoe* of God. Man could never be satisfied, and his continual search for what he had lost is recorded in the existence of religion wherever man is found.

Because man was created to share the *zoe* of God, he cannot be satisfied with the external rules and rituals of religion. He searched beyond the external and entered the world of the demonic, but that left him in bondage, fear and increased darkness. Only *zoe* will satisfy and fill the abyss within man's heart.

Jesus came, *zoe* in flesh. **In Him was life** *(zoe)*, **and the life** *(zoe)* **was the light of men** (John 1:4 NAS). In Acts 3:15 (NAS), He is called **the Prince of life** *(zoe)*. *The Amplified Bible* translates it as, **. . . the very Source — the Author — of life . . . .**

From the beginning of His ministry, it was apparent that He was saying something radically different from anything that had gone before. He continually assured His disciples that to believe upon Him would result in their receiving and participating in *zoe* or eternal life.

Early in His ministry He spoke to Nicodemus:

"... that whoever believes may in Him have eternal life *(zoe)*.

"For God so loved the world, that He gave His only begotten Son, that whoever believes in Him should not perish, but have eternal life *(zoe)*."

John 3:15,16 NAS

"He who believes in the Son has eternal life *(zoe)*; but he who does not obey the Son shall not see life *(zoe)*."

John 3:36 NAS

Speaking to the woman of Samaria, He said:

"... whoever drinks of the water that I shall give him shall never thirst; but the water that I shall give him shall become in him a well of water springing up to eternal life *(zoe)*."

John 4:14 NAS

He rebuked the Pharisees, saying, "... you are unwilling to come to Me, that you may have life" *(zoe)* (John 5:40 NAS).

After feeding the 5,000, He promised them the true bread. "... I am the bread of life *(zoe)*; he who comes to Me shall not hunger, and he who believes in Me shall never thirst" (John 6:35 NAS). When a person comes to Him, the abyss in his heart is filled.

On another occasion He said, ... "I am the light of the world; he who follows Me shall not walk in darkness, but shall have the light of life" *(zoe)* (John 8:12 NAS).

The Law, referring to the commandments of God, called for performance on the part of man when it said, ... "DO THIS AND YOU WILL LIVE" (Luke 10:28 NAS). Jesus' message was different. He said that man was to believe upon Him and, with God's life, he would live.

He said the same thing, in a different way, when He spoke to His disciples concerning the God-kind of love, *agape*.

"A new commandment I give to you, that you love one another, even as I have loved you, that you also love one another.

"By this all men will know that you are My disciples, if you have love one for another."

John 13:34,35 NAS

In these words and promises He was showing the nature of the salvation that He had come to accomplish. Calling men to participate in God's life and love took the matter beyond anything man could do in terms of achievement. No amount of dedication could produce in a man the nature of God! This is not a matter of Law that a man seeks to obey, but of the gift of Life out of which a new lifestyle spontaneously flows.

Jesus did not come merely to forgive us and send us on our way to do our best with His help to be good. Jesus came to begin a new race of people who shared in His *zoe*. This was, and still is, radical.

We are not talking of a person taking or not taking drugs or alcohol, or going to church on Sunday or dressing in a certain way. I am saying we are called to receive the life of God, *zoe*, into our lives, to become members of a new race of beings.

In John 12:24 (NAS), Jesus described how this gift was going to be made available to man.

"Truly, truly, I say to you, unless a grain of wheat falls into the earth and dies, it remains by itself alone; but if it dies, it bears much fruit."

It is obvious what Jesus is saying. Unless a seed is dropped into the ground to die, there will only be the one seed. In planting it in the ground, the miracle of the harvest happens and it produces many more exactly like itself.

Of all the seeds Jesus might have taken to illustrate this truth, He chose wheat. Wheat belongs to the one family of seeds that will always exactly reproduce the seed that was planted.

Jesus is describing Himself as the original seed; and through His death and resurrection, He will reproduce His life in millions who believe upon Him. It will not be a life like His — it will be nothing less than His very life lived in the believer!

When does God deal with our sin? When is this gift of *zoe*-life made available to us? It is not when we call upon Him, for it took place 2,000 years ago in the death, resurrection and ascension of Jesus!

Man's sin must be judged and put away. And man must:

be delivered from the power of the devil

be delivered from all the results of the fall

receive the gift of God's life

have the love of God poured out in his heart

regain his dominion to reign in life.

He can achieve none of this in his own worthiness or strength, for he is the helpless slave of sin and death. But God has done all of this for man, blessing him with all spiritual blessings, and He has done it in one Man.

The body of truth that we call the Gospel would be better understood as the Good News. News is the announcement of things that have taken place. The Gospel is the announcement of what God has perfectly done, achieving for us everything that we need.

The Gospel is not a call to do something, but the announcement that all is done in the One Who stood for all. This is the meaning behind the key expression in the New Testament, "in Christ." God put all men in the one Man and dealt with everyone, once and for all time, in Him.

This is difficult for our Western minds to grasp; but to the Hebrew mind, the idea of one standing for all was common. The story of David and his confrontation with Goliath illustrates this.

Two armies, the Philistines and the Israelites, face each other across the valley of Elah. It is going to be a decisive battle that affects every person in both nations. Goliath, the champion of the Philistine army, steps forward and challenges Israel to send out their champion to fight with him.

The idea was that, instead of wasting many men in a battle, let one man stand for the Philistines and another for the Israelites, and let the two of them fight. The man who is the victor wins for his nation. In fact, when they faced each other, the two men were no longer private citizens; they were the embodiment of their respective nations.

When David went to battle with Goliath, he was Israel. Every Israelite was "in David." His history was their history; what happened to him, happened to everyone. If he was defeated, all of Israel would become the slaves of Philistia.

As the soldiers of Israel watched David dance around Goliath, they knew that they too were out there on the side of the valley. His expertise with the slingshot became theirs as he, in their place and as them, whirled the sling around. When the monstrous man fell to the ground, they all knew the victory, felt the sword in their hands as his head was severed. They then went, proceeding from David's victory, to possess the land of the Philistines.

Jesus, the *zoe*, the Word through Whom all creation had leapt into being and was upheld, came to be the representative of the human race. It was because of Who He was that He could stand as each one of us. The Life that is the source and upholder of all life, can take the place of all His creation. He would be as us, bear the penalty of our sin, enter into our death, defeat all the powers that held us bound and rise as us triumphant.

This had never happened in the history of *zoe*! *Zoe* had created life out of nothing, but at the cross He entered into death, the unlife. He embraced death and was embraced by it, tasted it to the full and, having conquered it, returned alive.

The resurrection is a greater manifestation of the *zoe* of God than creation ever was. He is not only "the Life," but **. . . the resurrection and the life** . . . (John 11:25 NAS).

His resurrection meant that every sin that stood between man and God had been dealt with. It meant that death itself had died in the resurrection of Jesus. It meant that the devil lost all authority over the sons of men and was, therefore, defeated and helpless before any one of them. It meant that man was no longer held in the power of death, but was included in the resurrection and could now receive the *zoe*.

The risen Jesus is the focus of the Gospel. As we rest in what He has done, the Holy Spirit brings all that He has achieved into our experience.

He came to the disciples after He had risen and breathed into them, saying, **. . . "Receive the Holy Spirit"** (John 20:22 NAS). He who stood before them was the *zoe*-life Who had been through death and emerged the Conqueror.

He did it not only for us, but as us. Everything He achieved was now ours as surely as it was His. And He breathed His death-conquering life into those who believed upon Him, uniting Himself to them in so doing.

He, who stood objectively in front of them, now actually lived inside of them by His Spirit! A group of terrified, confused humans became one with the Life that had conquered death, devil and sin. From that moment, they lost all fear and entered into a relationship and fellowship with God that man had craved since the expulsion from Eden.

It was a new birth, the beginning of the new race. They had hung with Him on the cross and now, risen with Him, they lived in this new dimension of life. They would never again define life apart from Him. He had now become their *zoe*-life.

Paul summed it up with the words, **For to me, to live is Christ . . .** (Phil. 1:21 NAS) and **. . . Christ, who is our life** (*zoe*) **. . .** (Col. 3:4 NAS). And in Galatians 2:20 (NAS):

> **"I have been crucified with Christ; and it is no longer I who live, but Christ lives in me; and the life which I now live in the flesh I live by faith in the Son of God, who loved me, and delivered Himself up for me."**

Peter put it succinctly, **. . . that by them you might become partakers of the divine nature . . .** (2 Pet. 1:4 NAS).

The Gospel is not a call to imitate Jesus. The Good News is that, through participation in the resurrection event, I can now receive His life into me. From now on, He lives as me, without making me a puppet. In fact, He restores to me my freedom and meaning of existence.

The lifestyle of a believer is 100 percent supernatural. The behavior modification of religion does not approach the life portrayed in the New Testament. Knowing this, it stays with its frivolous externals and rituals, and avoids the unclimbable mountain of *zoe*.

That which man cannot achieve, we have as our possession, by God's grace . . . just because He loves us! We believe and rest in what He has done for us.

The virtues of the Christian life are clearly described as having their origin in the Spirit within. **But the fruit of the Spirit is love, joy, peace, patience, kindness, goodness, faithfulness, gentleness, self-control . . .** (Gal. 5:22,23 NAS).

The believer cannot be explained outside of the Spirit of Christ living within him. **. . . But if anyone does not have the Spirit of Christ, he does not belong to Him** (Rom. 8:9 NAS).

In this sense, there is no such thing as "Christian morality" that can be imposed on a city or nation. The Christian way of life cannot be formulated and handed out as guidelines for successful living. The Christian lifestyle was never thought of as having an existence apart from the living Christ Himself being its source at the heart of the believer.

When a believer burns out, it's his own human resources that have been exhausted. God's infinite *zoe* can never be depleted. If He lives in each of us and is our life, then spiritual burnout is caused by the believer's failure to rest in and receive the continual flow of His life.

When a branch burns, the flames feed on the gases that are locked up in the wood. As these gases are spent, the wood is reduced to ashes and the flames flicker and die. But there was once a bush that burned, and it was not consumed by the flames. As it blazed, the flames were not feeding on the resources of the bush; it was only the vehicle that contained and expressed the fire.

The flame and radiant light that came from the bush was the uncreated Life, the *zoe*, of God Who is Light. When the Presence of God departed from the bush, the leaves were green and the branches as moist as they had been before. It had burned, but none of its resources had been drawn upon.

The Christian life is not living in our own strength and resources, but from the infinite Christ Who lives within those who believe. All human strength will come to an end sooner or later, leaving each of us with a charred, burned out life. But His strength knows no end!

---

[1]W. E. Vine, *An Expository Dictionary of New Testament Words* (Old Tappan: Fleming H. Revell Co., 1966), p. 336.

Chapter 7

LIVING

THE LIFE OF CHRIST

We sat on the veranda and looked out across the clearing that was as big as a football field. We were in one of several western-style bungalows which were nestled among the trees on the perimeter of the compound. The missionary, an old friend from London, poured from a china teapot that a native had brought to us. A fan turned slowly overhead, stirring the humid air.

Sitting in a large rattan chair opposite me, he looked across the clearing that was the hub of the mission station. A piper cub was landing on the rough airstrip in the center of the field. Natives were busy herding cattle out of its path.

Finally, he turned and said, "I heard what you said this morning in the Bible study, Malcolm. I know that Christ lives in us, and I know that means the love of God is in us. I suppose, actually, that all Christians know it, but we dismiss it as a rather wonderful idea and leave it there. You know how we get around it!" he laughed.

"Positionally, we are in Christ in heavenly places, but actually I am down here slugging it out with my brothers. Somehow God sees us perfect, even though I know I am jolly well imperfect. I sometimes feel that if God knew me as well as I know me, He wouldn't say that I'm seated in heavenly places!" He laughed again, a hollow little laugh.

"Let's face it, Malcolm, if the life of Christ is within us, and if that life is love, why is it that however much I try to be like Jesus, I fall flat on my face? Let's be perfectly frank. There are five missionary couples on this station, two from the States and three from England. We are stuck out here in the middle of the bush, 500 miles from Monrovia, and what you see in front of you is our world.

"The only English-speaking white people I see in weeks and sometimes months are the other missionaries. And would you believe that we are hardly on speaking terms?

"The men are jealous of each other; the wives fight like cats and dogs and talk to each other only at the meetings; the children even fight! There is more resentment and bitterness right here that I have hours to tell you. And I am as guilty as any of them.

"Then of course, it comes between my wife and me. We argue about the arguments . . . you know, take sides over the latest fighting going on. I have already decided that I am not coming back for another term. How can I preach to the natives when it's not working in my own life? Or anybody else's life," he added moodily.

I have heard similar words on almost every mission field I have been. My heart breaks for these men and women who uprooted lives and family to take the Gospel to the ends of the earth . . . only to discover when they got there that they didn't know how to live what they were preaching!

I have sat with young missionaries in the Philippines, six months into their first term. They had left their Bible school with great words of faith, but rapidly discovered that they didn't know how to love as Jesus loved or live in the power of His resurrection life. They had come to the sickening realization that what they thought was faith was only brave, positive thinking.

And this is not a failure peculiar to missionaries. I have had the same conversation with housewives in Los Angeles, Wall Street executives and burned-out church-hoppers in Tulsa.

How does the *zoe*, the life of Christ Himself, actually become manifest in our lives? We know that to try and imitate it in our own strength is utter despair. But then, how *does* He live through us?

Some of the most important words Jesus spoke to His disciples were at the supper the night before He suffered and died. The disciples were confused and full of questions; they had no idea of what was transpiring. They didn't realize they were living through minutes of history that were to usher in the New Covenant, bringing man to God.

They still clung to the Jewish idea that the Messiah was going to set up a throne in Jerusalem and conquer His enemies. They saw themselves as the members of Messiah's cabinet. On their way to supper they had been arguing bitterly among themselves as to who was the greatest, who would have first place in the kingdom which they felt, most surely, would arrive that weekend.

Jesus had shocked them at the very beginning of the meal by taking the place of the lowest slave and washing their feet, hardly the action of a powerful world ruler! He had then spoken of them loving one another with His kind of love . . . *agape.*

> **"A new commandment I give to you, that you love one another, even as I have loved you, that you also love one another.**
>
> **"By this all men will know that you are My disciples, if you have love for one another."**
>
> **John 13:34,35** NAS

How could these power-hungry disciples, jostling for place and jealous of each other's position in the disciple band, ever be part of a kingdom where all would serve and love one another even as Jesus?

Jesus further confused them by saying, **"In that day you shall know that I am in My Father, and you in Me, and I in you"** (John 14:20 NAS).

Back in Galilee, He had come to them as they were mending their nets, and said, **"Follow Me!"** And they had left their fishing business and followed Him down the roads of Israel. They had sat and listened by the hour to what He said; they had watched as He healed the sick.

He was their teacher and they were His disciples. The same as the disciples of other great rabbis, they sat at His feet to learn from Him, seeking to put His teaching into practice.

But now He was speaking in concepts that confused them. How could this Person, Who was sitting in front of them, come and be inside of them? And how, at the same time, could they be in Him? There was no category in their minds or wildest imaginations to contain the idea.

The Old Covenant dealt with the Law, its commands and rituals. One learned from the teacher how things should be done, and then went ahead and tried to practice what had been heard.

Jesus was saying that, in the new day that would dawn in His resurrection, there would not be a new codified Law that everyone would have to learn and try to do. He himself would be the new Law! He did not give them teaching to learn, because He was not only the Teacher, but also the teaching. He had said, . . . **"I am the . . . truth . . ."** (John 14:6 NAS).

The new Law of loving one another with God's kind of love was not an exterior command, but Love Himself living within them. He would live at the source of their beings, in their "want to's," and their lives would be an expression of Him.

Sensing their confusion, He went on to give them an illustration:

"I am the true vine, and My Father is the vinedresser.

"Every branch in Me that does not bear fruit, He takes away; and every branch that bears fruit, He prunes it, that it may bear more fruit.

"You are already clean because of the word which I have spoken to you.

"Abide in Me, and I in you. As the branch cannot bear fruit of itself, unless it abides in the vine, so neither can you, unless you abide in Me.

"I am the vine, you are the branches; he who abides in Me, and I in Him, he bears much fruit; for apart from Me you can do nothing."

John 15:1-5 NAS

He calls Himself, "the Vine." When we say "vine," we mean the vine life, the unique sap that causes the vine to look the way it does, to bear the leaves, blossoms and grapes that it does. Jesus is saying that He is the life that makes a believer who he is, and the believer's lifestyle is His life in manifestation.

The believer is the branch within the vine. It is interesting that out of all the woods that were available, Jesus chose the vine. The wood of the vine is totally useless for anything except bearing grapes. No furniture can be made from its wood; it's not used for carving.

Jesus was telling us that we have one function in life: to be the manifestors of His life to the world. Only when we are living His life are we truly living our own! This is the reason for our creation.

The disciples were looking at Messiah's reign as an organization with positions to be filled, territories to be carved. Jesus was saying that, although that is true in the world, it is not so with Him. His reign, that was about to burst upon the world, would be Himself expressed through millions of believers. He would no longer be limited in geography, but would be present wherever one of His branches would let Him bear fruit.

By calling believers branches, He showed their inability to produce fruit by themselves. A branch severed from the flow of the vine life cannot produce a leaf or a single grape. It is the rising vine life sap that flows through the branch and, through it, produces the fruit. In union with the vine life, the branch can do what branches cannot do!

It is only for the sake of analysis that we speak of vine and branches. When we look at a vine, the two are one. Whoever heard of a vine without branches . . . whoever called a heap of dead wood a vine?

Jesus is saying that the believer does not have an independent existence that every so often must receive special help, a spiritual boost, in order to continue in his Christian life. The vine branch cannot be thought of apart from the life flowing through it, and a believer cannot be thought of except as an expression of Christ Jesus.

Likewise, the only way Jesus is known on earth today is through His branch-believers. His life must have a channel through which to flow to the world.

This relationship never changes. We are always the branch, and He is always the life that produces the fruit through us . . . so do not be shattered when you feel the helplessness of being a branch.

Faced with a challenge or opportunity to express divine love, we feel a keen sense of helplessness, a lack of ability to be or do what the situation demands. When temptation calls, we find a drawing within us to respond. That is not sin! We are simply feeling our "branchness" and realizing that Jesus was right when He said, "Without Me you can do nothing."

Growing up as a believer does not mean that gradually we become so Christ-like in ourselves that we will one day bear fruit on our own — and Jesus will be proud of us. We will always be branches that are helpless apart from the vine life that flows through us.

When we feel our weakness, the impossibility of living Christ in this or that situation, it is the way it should be. We are forever the helpless branches, and He is forever the vine life. We do not struggle to be the Christian we think the situation demands . . . nor do we bemoan to God our weakness. We deliberately recognize that Christ lives at the source of our being, and we choose to let Him live through and as us at the point of our weakness.

To religion, this is baffling. Religion always thinks of God in terms of separation. He is the "over there" God who lives in a temple; He is the sky God, far away. We pray in order to get His help for our situation.

Jesus, risen from the dead, has brought about an entirely new situation that is unique in the world. He rose from the dead; and now by the Spirit, He is not confined to a geography, but is intimately present within the heart of every believer. We can no more think of ourselves as being separate from Him, than a branch bearing grapes can think of itself as separate from the vine life.

Paul illustrated the relationship between Christ and the believer by the union of a head with the body. We cannot think of the head as being separate from a living body, the two are functionally one. To think of my head being English, while my body is French, is foolishness. So is the idea that my head is a millionaire while my body is a pauper. What is true of the head is also true of the body. In the same way, the believer is joined with Christ.

He is not "over there" to be called to "come over here" and help me when I am tempted or face an opportunity or challenge. He is one with my spirit, and my realization of weakness is but the trigger to let Him answer the situation with His *zoe*-life through me.

Paul spoke plainly of this in Galatians 2:20 (NAS), **"I have been crucified with Christ; and it is no longer I who live, but Christ lives in me . . . ."**; and in Ephesians 3:17 (NAS), **. . . that Christ may dwell in your hearts through faith . . . .**; and in Colossians 1:27 (NAS), **. . . Christ in you, the hope of glory.**

He summed up the secret of his whole life in Philippians 4:11-13 (NAS):

> **. . . I have learned to be content in whatever circumstances I am.**
>
> **I know how to get along with humble means, and I also know how to live in prosperity; in any and every circumstance I have learned the secret of being filled and going hungry, both of having abundance and suffering need.**
>
> **I can do all things through Him who strengthens me.**

His ability to handle whatever circumstance he found himself in did not arise from his having a stoic personality. He lived as he did because of **. . . Him who strengthens me** (v. 13). *The Amplified Bible* translation throws light on what he means:

> **I have strength for all things in Christ Who empowers me — I am ready for anything and equal to anything through Him Who infuses inner strength into me, [that is, I am self-sufficient in Christ's sufficiency].**
>
> **Philippians 4:13 AMP**

The word *infuse* means "to steep, soak, so as to extract certain qualities." One day, a number of years ago, I sat in a diner pondering these great truths. I asked myself, "How can Christ, the *zoe-agape* of God live in me?"

The waitress brought me a cup of hot water with a tea bag on the side. I began dipping the tea bag into the water, watching it turn color as it received the strength of the tea. I removed the tea bag still full of the tea leaves, and proceeded to drink my cup of tea.

Suddenly, it dawned on me that I had just "infused" the tea into the water — giving me a refreshing cup of tea. The strength and taste of the tea had been released from the tea leaves into the colorless, tasteless water. The tasteless water was the necessary vehicle to release the taste of the tea.

Laying the tea bag against the cup would never do it! Water cannot imitate tea by looking at it! There had to be an infusion. I realized then that I, in myself, was impotent to reproduce the life of Christ, even as the water was helpless to turn itself into tea. If I was to live His life, then He must come and live it within me. His life must be infused into my spirit.

If the resurrected Jesus is going to be known and tasted by the world today, it is not as a result of man trying to be like Him, but of Him being expressed through our weakness. The tea will always be locked up in the bag until released through the medium of the water.

The fusion of the tea and water is so complete that we no longer call it water, but tea. Yet, it is not, for the tea is still in the bag. So Christ is in us, our life is His life, yet He has not become us and we have not become Him. We are forever distinct, and forever one.

This is the miracle that takes place when a person comes to Christ. The Spirit of Christ comes into him.

On the night of the resurrection, Jesus stood objectively in front of the disciples; and yet at the same time, He was within them as He breathed Himself into their spirits. So when a person calls upon Jesus, He comes within. **. . . If anyone does not have the Spirit of Christ, he does not belong to Him** (Rom. 8:9 NAS).

The believer is a Christ-inside person! To speak of a believer without the Spirit of Christ is a misnomer, for such a person does not exist.

> **. . . Do you not yourselves realize and know (thoroughly by an ever-increasing experience) that Jesus Christ is in you? unless you are [counterfeits] disapproved on trial and rejected!**
>
> **2 Corinthians 13:5 AMP**

The extent to which this can be realized in our lives is unlimited! The New Testament makes it clear that the fullness of God now dwells in us. **For in Him all the fullness of Deity dwells in bodily form, and in Him you have been made complete . . .** (Col. 2:9,10 NAS).

The Amplified Bible renders verse 10:

73

> **And you are in Him, made full and have come to fullness of life**
> **— in Christ you too are filled with the Godhead; Father, Son and**
> **Holy Spirit, and reach full spiritual stature . . . .**

Because this is the true status of a believer, Paul prays that it may actually become so in their life and experience: **. . . that you may be filled up to all the fullness of God** (Eph. 3:19 NAS).

The Amplified Bible translates it:

> **. . . that you may be filled (through all your being) unto all the**
> **fullness of God — (that is) may have the richest measure of the**
> **divine Presence, and become a body wholly filled and flooded with**
> **God Himself!**
>
>

Ephesians 3:19 AMP
>

When we live from the fullness of Christ living within us, we cannot burn out.

Chapter 8

TRUE FAITH

One of the major causes of spiritual burnout is the distortion of our faith by the leaven of the Pharisees. We live by faith, and when it is turned into a work of the flesh, spiritual exhaustion is inevitable.

What do we mean when we use the word *faith*? It is vital we understand exactly what we mean, because a slight distortion in our definition will mean chaos and disaster further down the road.

Faith is essentially a trust response to a given set of facts. Our faith in relationship to God can be illustrated to some degree on the human level.

Let us suppose I met a person who freely opened his heart to me, and showed himself to be good and kind to the extreme. Suppose he went further and acted toward me in ways that concretely showed his goodness. And let's further suppose, he committed himself to me with the promise that, according to his ability, he would be all a friend could be for the rest of my life.

Such action demands some kind of response. I could, of course, be suspicious that he had ulterior motives and walk away congratulating myself that I didn't get caught. Or, I could take a risk and respond to his words and actions with trust, believing him to be all he claimed to be. That is, to have faith in him and allow him to make good all of his intentions. Actually, my faith would be permission to let him express the love and kindness he said he wanted to give.

There is a certain risk attached to this kind of a commitment that will be tried over the years. There may be times when what I see and hear might suggest that he is not all that he had seemed to be; but the nature of faith is that, having committed itself, it then tenaciously rests in the character of the man as I know him — rather than what I am presently seeing.

My response to him would cause the beginning of a bonding together of our spirits that would mature over the years into true friendship. Such a human relationship is a shadow of the place faith has in our relationship with God.

Faith does not start with man. Our faith begins with God opening His heart to us; He reveals His love and grace that He has made concrete in Jesus. It begins with God's character and what He has done for us in Christ. Faith's first action is a trusting response to the revelation God has given.

God has revealed Himself in His Word, but faith is given when the Holy Spirit makes that Word alive to us personally. **So faith comes from hearing, and hearing by the word of Christ** (Rom. 10:17 NAS). The Greek for *word* is *rhema*, which means this verse could be translated, ". . . hearing the word from the lips of Jesus Himself."

Faith is a response to something or someone outside of itself — in this case, the revelation of God in Jesus and His faithfulness to that revelation. The response takes the form of opening the door to allow God in Christ to be all He has promised; it is letting God be the God He says He is in any given situation.

Faith could be likened to the eye of the spirit that, beholding Jesus, is awakened to respond to Him, rest in Him and allow Him to be all He has revealed Himself to be. In the same way, it is the ear of the spirit that, upon hearing His Word, is excited to rest in Him and let Him be all He has declared Himself to be.

In ourselves, we have no faith that can please God. The faith that we have in Him comes from Him! Explaining the way the lame man was healed at the Beautiful Gate, Peter said, "**. . . the faith which comes through Him has given him this perfect health in the presence of you all**" (Acts 3:16 NAS). *The New English Bible* renders it, **. . . the name of Jesus, by awakening faith . . . .**

There is no struggle trying to have enough faith to meet a problem situation, for faith does not come from who we are but Who He is. **. . . run with endurance the race that is set before us, fixing our eyes on Jesus, the author and perfecter of faith . . .** (Heb. 12:1,2 NAS).

The Greek word for *author* would be better translated *source*. Our faith finds its source in Who He is, and finds its strength in His faithfulness to His Word.

We must not think that hearing the faith-producing Word means treating the Bible like a textbook and selecting the appropriate passage. The Holy Spirit must take the truths of Scripture and make them real in the heart. So when Paul preached, he depended completely on the Holy Spirit to make the Word real so people's faith would be true, saving faith.

> **And my message and my preaching were not in persuasive words of wisdom, but in demonstration of the Spirit and of power, that your faith should not rest on the wisdom of men, but on the power of God.**
>
> **1 Corinthians 2:4 NAS**

After Paul left an area, he never ceased to pray for the believers there that the revelation of God's heart and character would continue to be given.

> **(I) do not cease giving thanks for you, while making mention of you in my prayers;**
>
> **that the God of our Lord Jesus Christ, the Father of glory, may give to you a spirit of wisdom and of revelation in the knowledge of Him.**
>
> **Ephesians 1:16,17 NAS**

Faith cannot be born based on what God has done for someone else. He must speak His Word in our hearts, which will leave us not with a true fact in our head, but with an absolute knowledge in our hearts.

The revelation that we receive is focused in the death and resurrection of Jesus. It is here that God has revealed Himself. The Holy Spirit witnesses that Jesus is really alive; even the first preachers knew that, unless He witnessed to the truth of Jesus being alive, no one would believe a word they said! **"And we are witnesses of these things; and so is the Holy Spirit, whom God has given to those who obey Him"** (Acts 5:32 NAS).

Faith is man's abandonment to and rest in God's revelation. The Hebrew word for *trust* has in it the idea of falling flat on the face, without support. Faith is a person's dropping the weight of his life — past, present and future — onto the revelation that Jesus is alive.

Faith, by its very nature, is a commitment to what we have now seen and heard, a burning of bridges behind us . . . walking into the unknown future having staked all on the resurrection of Jesus from the dead.

From the moment of commitment, the language and actions of the believer reflect his rest of faith.

One bitterly cold January morning, I left New York's JFK airport, dressed in a light, summer suit. The reason for my apparent insanity was that I would be disembarking in Johannesburg, South Africa, where it would be summer. My summer outfit did not create the hot weather in Africa; I was dressed because it was summer there. Faith does not confess in order to create God's blessing; it confesses because it sees the blessing is there already in Christ.

Because we know in our hearts, our actions and the words of our lips fall in line with what our hearts have seen. Many times, what we have come to see as final truth conflicts with our feelings and with appearances. The world mocks us as crazy because they do not see what we see, but we have seen with the eye of faith, and that must result in the bold confession of faith before the watching world.

> . . . the word of faith which we are preaching, that if you confess with your mouth Jesus as Lord, and believe in your heart that God raised Him from the dead, you shall be saved.
>
> **Romans 10:8,9** NAS

The act of faith does not save, heal or bless us, but it is the means by which God does within us that which He desires. It allows Him to walk into our life with all the blessings He has covenanted for us in Christ.

As faith thus responds, the Spirit witnesses with our spirits that the matter is done; and we "know that we know" we are united to God in Christ. Galatians 4:6 (NAS) says, **And because you are sons, God has sent forth the Spirit of His Son into our hearts, crying, "Abba! Father!"** And in 1 John 4:16 (NAS), **And we have come to know and have believed the love which God has for us . . . .**

Every step of our life in Christ is taken by faith after the same pattern that was first manifested at salvation. Always, there is the word from God, made alive to us from the written Word by the Spirit, the revelation of Him in our present circumstance. This is followed by our trusting, expectant response and rest in Him, allowing Him to accomplish His Word in and by us.

An expression in the Old Testament described faith as "waiting on the Lord." Isaiah described how faith was the means of revitalizing burned out believers.

> **"Do you not know? Have you not heard? The everlasting God, the Lord, the Creator of the ends of the earth does not become weary or tired . . .**
>
> **He gives strength to the weary and to him who lacks might He increases power.**
>
> **Though youths grow weary and tired, and vigorous young men stumble badly, yet those who wait for the Lord will gain new strength; they will mount up with wings like eagles, they will run and not get tired, they will walk and not become weary."**
>
> **Isaiah 40:28-31** NAS

The word Isaiah uses for *youths* describes the very best of physical strength, a candidate for the Olympics. The very best of natural strength will one day come to the end of its endurance and fall weary on the side of the road.

Over against that, he places the infinite strength of the Eternal God and states that those who wait upon Him will live in His limitless strength while walking through the pressures of this life.

The word *wait* contained the idea of looking to the revelation God had given and expecting Him to be all that He had promised. But the word also means that the one who looks is braided together with or made a unity with the object he is looking at.

As faith looks and commits to all that God has revealed Himself to be, human weakness is swallowed up and becomes one with divine strength. An exchange takes place — in the place of our human strength there now flows His divine! In that exchange, the believer can fly like an eagle, run forever in a strength beyond his own, and even walk through the mundane every day of life without falling down.

The belief system of the Pharisee has distorted faith into a work, one of the rungs of the ladder by which religion seeks to climb to God. In one sense, for the legalist, it is the ultimate rung of the ladder, for without faith there can be no pleasing God. (Heb. 11:6.) If faith is a work by which we gain God's acceptance, then to have faith is to have made it!

Legalistic faith is subtle. Defined in a word, it is "faith in faith in God!" Instead of the Object Who is the Source and Sustainer of faith, the emphasis is on the faith itself. It becomes a strained effort to get it, keep it and grow it.

The accent is on the words that are said, the mental attitude that is rigorously held. It leans heavily on the true faith that is seen and reported in others, rather than a personal word from God. The feeling is, if the formula worked for one, it will work for another.

It produces not only the strain that is always associated with the works of the flesh, but also a constant fear lest it should be lost, and condemnation should one not seem to have enough. It is here that thousands drop out spiritually exhausted . . . because they do not have the faith that is birthed out of a revelation, but from a dead formula handed to them by religion.

Because the focus is on the faith itself rather than on the God who awakens faith, this pseudo-faith seeks to manipulate God. Once it is accepted that faith is a power that I can use to influence God, it is only one more step to thinking of it as the currency of heaven with which I can purchase any blessing from God.

We do not come to God saying, "Do this for me because of my faith." Faith is unconscious of itself and says, "Do this for me because of Who You have shown Yourself to be!"

The exhaustion that comes from trying to make God do our will leaves people not only burned out, but also disillusioned and bitter. They feel that God did not honor the currency they laid on His counter.

The simple commitment that true faith makes changes everything. Never again will there be the struggle to have enough faith. Whether for healing, for a greater experience of the Spirit, for needs to be met or for an answer to prayer, faith simply responds to Who He is now and lets Him come into the situation. He is the healer and the source of all blessings.

Seeing Him, the answer to all needs and desires, the believer responds, "Lord Jesus, all of this You are now to me!"

Chapter 9

THE REST OF FAITH

We know that the inexhaustable life that rose out of death is available for us so that we might live triumphantly in this present world. But how do we get that life into our own weak lives? God's infinite wisdom is within Himself, but we need His wisdom to walk through the problems and confusions of our lives.

Facing the hurts in the lives of people all around us, we feel callous and uncaring. How do we get His compassion into our hearts? When others hurt us and we find no ability within ourselves to love and forgive them, how can we get His divine, forgiving love into our hearts?

The answer religion gives to this is always in terms of something we do. In my youth, I asked that question of many pastors and always the answer was a variation on the same idea. To have the flow of the life of God, one must set aside time to pray and read the Bible on a regular basis; our quiet hour with God is the key to abiding in Christ.

I do not believe this is true. In fact, I believe it only adds to the problem and increases the frustration. There are many reasons to set aside quality time with God; but if we are doing it in order to get the flow of God into our lives, we are only adding to our spiritual exhaustion.

To say that the life of Christ flows in and through our lives because we spend an hour in devotion today, is to turn prayer and Bible study into a work of the flesh. It is to make the activity one more rung on the ladder to God.

The Pharisees pored over the Scripture and said prayers believing that, in this way, they would somehow tap into God's life. Jesus plainly told them that in so doing they were missing the only source of life which is Christ himself.

"You search the Scriptures, because you think that in them you have eternal life; and it is these that bear witness of Me;

and you are unwilling to come to Me, that you may have life."

John 5:39,40 NAS

Similarly, dedications, promises and vows to God that our life will be completely His from now on fall into the same category. How dedicated must a person be before the life begins to flow? What level of being "sold out to God" must we be at before the first trickle of the *zoe* begins to come? All of these works will only hurry a person along the slippery road of burnout.

In Colossians 2:6 (NAS), Paul tells us how to abide and walk daily in Christ: **As you therefore have received Christ Jesus the Lord, so walk in Him.**

We received Him by faith and, in the same way, we abide in Him and express Him to the world. Paul spelled out what he was praying for the Ephesians. **May Christ through your faith [actually] dwell — settle down, abide, make His permanent home — in your hearts!** . . . (Eph. 3:17 AMP).

Minute by minute, we live by faith in His ability within us. In this way, the divine energy of His love is released through us into every situation in which we find ourselves.

We have come to the very heart of the Good News; it is faith and not works! In the New Testament, to accept the Gospel was seen to be an obedience of faith. That is, a response to and rest in the Christ Who had become their Savior and Life . . . not obedience to rules imposed by man. It is not even obedience to the Ten Commandments, but the obedience that arises from faith:

. . . obedience of faith.

Romans 16:26 NAS

. . . we have received grace and apostleship to bring about the obedience of faith among all the Gentiles . . . .

Romans 1:5 NAS

. . . a great many of the priests were becoming obedient to the faith.

Acts 6:7 NAS

It is at this point that a believer, burning out in his efforts to please God, moves from exhaustion to rest. Tired and wearied with his struggle to perform acceptably for God through the disciplines and dedications of religion, he hears the grace of God and the Holy Spirit makes it alive in his heart.

Like the returning son in Jesus' story, most of us see very little of what God desires to give us. We are perfectly happy to come home at the level of a hired servant; we feel that the slave position is appropriate for us. If we can be forgiven and continue to receive forgiveness, we feel we can ask no more.

Faith is a response, and so it can only respond to the level it has seen and heard. It is after we have come home that we discover the Father's grace is infinitely greater than we had ever dreamed, and our faith responds to the increased revelation.

We realize that He is not only the past tense Savior from sin, but the One Who now lives within us in the present tense, our life and breath. Christianity is not a formula, but the Person of Jesus Himself.

Seeing that He is within, faith responds and allows that fact to invade all of life. Regardless of feelings and appearances, faith holds to the Word of God and declares that Christ is living within.

This simple commitment changes everything. Never again will the believer try to be like Jesus; the revelation of Christ living within has rescued him from religious ladder climbing. He no longer tries to live for God, he lives from Him Who is the source of his life.

When doubts arise, faith does not panic. It simply turns to Him Who is the source and perfecter of our faith, knowing that He is committed to His Word in this situation.

The Scripture is not a book of systematic theology that tabulates what we are to believe. It is a book of biographies that show how very ordinary people through the ages have learned to walk in God's strength to overcome their problems. In telling their stories, the Holy Spirit holds nothing back. He shows how they discovered the reality of God in the black holes of their personal failures.

Many of them illustrate exactly how they found the answer to the question we are posing. How does a person get the life of God to flow into his life? How does a person become a functioning branch in the vine?

David was such a person and, because we know more of the inner workings of his heart than any other character in the Scriptures, he is an excellent model to study. In David's psalms, his every spiritual mood is open for us to see and study.

Again and again, David was brought to face and deeply feel his own human weakness and inability to handle situations in life. He was unjustly accused, relentlessly pursued by a king who was insanely jealous of him, betrayed by people he thought were his friends . . . as well as having to deal with all his own sins and failures in life.

The amazing thing is . . . he never burned out! He freely expressed his feelings in the midst of all that went on, and they show a man in real distress.

And my soul is greatly dismayed; . . . I am weary with my sighing;
Every night I make my bed swim,

I dissolve my couch with my tears.

My eye has wasted away with grief . . . .

Psalm 6:3,6 NAS

O Lord, how my adversaries have increased!

Many are rising up against me. Many are saying of my soul, "There is no deliverance for him in God."

Psalm 3:1,2 NAS

. . . For the waters have threatened my life. I have sunk in deep mire, and there is no foothold; I have come into deep waters, and a flood overflows me. I am weary with my crying; my throat is parched . . . . Those who hate me without a cause are more than the hairs of my head . . . .

Psalm 69:1-4 NAS

. . . I am restless in my complaint and am surely distracted, because of the voice of the enemy, because of the pressure of the wicked; for they bring down trouble upon me, and in anger they bear a grudge against me.

My heart is in anguish within me, and the terrors of death have fallen upon me.

Fear and trembling come upon me; and horror has overwhelmed me.

And I said, "Oh, that I had wings like a dove! I would fly away and be at rest.

"Behold, I would wander far away, I would lodge in the wilderness.

"I would hasten to my place of refuge from the stormy wind and tempest."

Psalm 55:2-8 NAS

So that we can trace exactly how he went through pressure without having his spiritual strength sucked out of him, one of the times of deep distress that David went through is recorded in detail.

David and his men were living at this time in a remote wilderness town of Ziklag. They had been away for a number of days and were now returning home. As they came within sight of their town, they saw wisps of smoke in the sky and birds of prey circling high above. A few minutes later, they stood in the smoking ashes of what had once been their home.

In their absence, a passing band of Amalekites had plundered and left. Everything was gone, their families kidnapped, their homes burned to the ground.

It was too much. The strong men began to cry and David sobbed along with them. They cried until they could cry no more, and then sat in the ruins of their smoking homes, their feet in the warm ashes.

One by one, they began to express their feelings to each other. Someone was to blame for this outrage . . . someone had to pay. With wild rage in their eyes, one by one, they began to look toward David. Their looks said, "You brought us here, you will pay for this." It was a lynch mob in the making.

> **Then David and the people . . . lifted their voices and wept until there was no more strength in them to weep . . . .**

> **Moreover David was greatly distressed because the people spoke of stoning him, for all the people were embittered . . . But David strengthened himself in the Lord his God.**

> **1 Samuel 30:4,6 NAS**

The reason David does not burn out is in the words "strengthened himself." Literally translated, they mean he "bound himself together; pulled himself tight" — as in a tightened muscle. The expression also translates the idea of binding together and is used to describe Absolom's hair being "caught fast" in the branches of a tree. (2 Sam. 18:9.)

It should be noted that it is not in the passive tense. It is not that David "was strengthened," but that he "strengthened himself." Walking in the faith that abides in the vine is not being a robot waiting passively for God to act for us. It is not whimpering to a "separated God," asking Him to come and do something.

Another way this could be translated is, "David took courage." Divine courage and strength was there waiting for faith to take, and David took it. Here was a man on the verge of mental, emotional and spiritual burnout who, by the exercise of faith, pulled himself together . . . and so strengthened himself in the Lord.

What did he see in the Lord that pulled him together like a tight muscle? He went to the only Word of God he had, the first five books of our Bible. It was the manuscript of the covenant and outlined all God had revealed of Himself, all He had promised to those who believed.

It was from this same covenant book that David had learned while he was yet a baby in his mother's arms. As a teenager, alone in the wilderness with his sheep, he had studied, memorized and meditated on its words until they were part of him.

It clearly stated that God was the Rock of His people. (Deut. 32:4,30,31.) He was their Shepherd (Gen. 49:24); He guided them through the trackless wilderness with a pillar of cloud and fire (Ex. 13:21,22); He fed them every morning with bread from heaven. (Ex. 16:35.)

Through the exhibition of His power in the judgments He inflicted upon Egypt (Ex. 7-11) and the dividing of the Red Sea (Ex. 14), He established Himself as the Deliverer and Savior of His people from all their physical and spiritual enemies. When their Egyptian enemies were almost upon them, He became their Shield and Defense by putting the cloud of His Presence between them and their enemies. (Ex. 14:19,20.)

He had revealed Himself in His Names. He was *Yahweh Jireh*, the One Who promised that He would always be there to meet their needs. (Gen. 22:14.) He was *Yahweh Ropha* Who promised to heal all of their diseases and was, in fact, their daily health. (Ex. 15:26.) He was *Yahweh Nissi*, the God Who was Himself their banner under which He was their victory over all their enemies. (Ex. 17:15.)

All of this had been sworn in a blood covenant oath a thousand years before David was born, but David knew that his covenant God never changed. All He had revealed Himself to be to

Abraham, Moses and the ancient people of God, He was that forever.

But the people of Israel had long forgotten that their God was the living God; they had paralyzed their covenant into a religion. Most of them were spiritually burned out and exhausted.

David had never had a role model showing him how a man lived as a branch in the vine with his God . . . not even in his own family. Anyone in his family would have assured him that all the covenant stories were true, but they would have told him they were history from another age . . . things were different now.

While meditating on the Scriptures, in the wilderness with his sheep, David's eyes were opened by the Holy Spirit to see that the revelation God had given of Himself was still true. God waited for someone to respond with faith, allowing Him to enter his life and be to him all He had committed Himself to be.

In the last years through all his troubles, and now in the horror of Ziklag, David "strengthened himself in the Lord." He considered all that God had said He would be, and his faith responded to that revelation, rested in it, allowed God to be that to him. Faith caused him to be caught up into it, entwined and united with the God he had met in the revelation contained in the Scriptures.

The leap of faith took place when he said, "The Lord is my . . . ." From the period of his life when he was pressured with his worst troubles come some of his greatest psalms. They hinge on this expression of faith with which he united with God in his experience. The Lord was not simply the Shepherd of Israel, but **The Lord is *my* shepherd** . . . (Ps. 23:1 NAS). He was not merely the Salvation of His people. David said, **The Lord is *my* light and *my* salvation** . . . (Ps. 27:1 NAS).

Whatever God had declared Himself to be, David took Him for his own: "The Lord is the Defense of my life, . . . my Rock, . . . my Fortress, . . . my Deliverer, . . . my Shield, . . . my Stronghold."

He saw that God was all of this to him personally. He realized that he, the human — failing, weak and frightened — was united as one with God Himself. All that He had declared Himself to be to His covenant people, He was that to David — as if he was the only one in the covenant!

Note carefully exactly what David did in this situation. He did not set aside time to read the Scriptures, as if he believed that activity would produce the needed help. Nor did he pray!

To have prayed would have been to ask God to become, at some point in the future, what he needed Him to be right now. What he did was to boldly lay hold of all God had revealed Himself to be and said, "He is this — now!"

David focused his faith to the specific need or challenge that was confronting him. If he felt his need for guidance and wisdom in the trackless desert of life, his faith said, **The Lord is my shepherd** . . . (Ps. 23:1 NAS). If he was surrounded by enemies that threatened to exterminate him, he rested with the words, **. . . The Lord is the defense of my life; whom shall I dread?** (Ps. 27:1 NAS).

The need, the negative feelings, the darkness became the necessary trigger that released faith to rest in God, the specific answer. In that release of faith, David became consciously united to God. The Infinite Strength was now "*my* strength"; God Who is Light, was now "*my* light." Two, literally, have become one.

In the last years, I have spoken with hundreds of burned-out, disillusioned people who have prayed and looked for their lives to be changed. However, the emphasis of the Scriptures is not so much on change, but *exchange*!

As faith waits upon the Lord, the believer's weakness is swallowed up in His divine strength. The sap flows through the branch and His fruit is seen in our lives.

Our faith has a clearer vision of God than David ever had. We are members of a "better covenant" that has "better promises." He only had the revelation of God from Genesis to Deuteronomy. We have the fullest, final revelation, the Word Himself, Christ Jesus.

David understood his union with God through the shadows of the Old Testament covenants; but the God David knew from afar, entered into our humanity, died for us and rose out of death that He might by the Spirit live within us.

When troubles come, when faced with opportunities to be God's love to others, we feel our weakness and do not feel like great men of God. Many times we feel like David . . . weeping until we have no strength left.

Religion calls us to bemoan our weakness, dedicate and rededicate ourselves to try and find strength within us for the battle. Trying to find the ultimate dedication or experience that will change us into strong men of God, will only bring guilt and increase our spiritual exhaustion.

Our feelings are the necessary trigger for faith to replace our weakness with His strength. We can now understand Paul's triumphant statement, **. . . when I am weak, then I am strong** (2 Cor. 12:10 NAS).

A fantasy illustration might help at this point. Let us suppose I want to learn the game of tennis. I go to the bookstore and purchase all the books I can that explain the game, outlining the rules and showing how the game is played.

For days, I pore over the books, memorizing the rules and some of the plays. I stand awkwardly in my living room and hold my arms in the positions shown in the pictures. Convinced I am ready to play, I purchase a tennis outfit, a racquet and some balls and head for the tennis courts.

Very quickly, I discover that, in spite of all the hours I have spent studying the game, when it comes to playing, I know nothing! My muscles refuse to cooperate and the balls fly everywhere — except the place I want them to go.

Having made a complete fool of myself, I slink off the court and return to my books. But every time I try to play again, it seems to get worse. In fact, the harder I try, the more tense I am and the worse my feeble attempts become.

I study the games of past players and even go to Wimbledon to watch the world champions play. When I come home, my pathetic attempts to hit the ball only announce to the world that I still cannot play tennis. Finally, I hire a coach who is a world champion. I listen to him and marvel at his ability; but when I try to do as he says and imitate his moves, something inside of me refuses to cooperate.

I have been trying to learn to play by the rules and regulations, taking instructions from books and people, coupled with my efforts to put it all into practice.

In fantasy, let's suppose I could invite the coach to actually step inside of me, into my mind, nerves and muscles. He would be within me, so he could think his thoughts in my head and let his muscles be my muscles, his memory of all his winning plays would be part of my memory . . . and yet, never take away my personality and freedom of choice.

I would be me and he would be himself — yet we would operate as one person. My part would be to give up trying to play tennis and admit my helplessness. I would have to understand that, if I insisted on trying to play, then the champion within me would let me return to my bumbling and making a fool of myself; the two of us could not play at the same time.

Standing on the court, freely admitting that I can't play, I choose to hand over to him. He plays, but I am choosing to let him. I begin to win all the games!

My coach did not teach me to play the game. If questioned, I would have to say, "The coach is my game." I now find myself doing everything the books had told me to do, the rules had demanded and my coach had ever taught me. But I am not doing it in my own ability, but by resting in the coach, who is the books and rules wrapped up in a person.

So Christ Jesus, by His Spirit, lives within us. The rest of faith is when we choose to let Him play the game of life in and as us. It is one leap of faith that declares He is our life and, later, a million choices of faith as every challenge is presented.

He produces in us everything the Law and all the stepladders of religion were aiming at — Love, which is the fulfilling of the Law. (Gal. 5:14.)

Chapter 10

OVERCOMING TEMPTATION

There is a certain euphoria that follows the discovery of what it means to be in Christ. With the rest that the believer has when he ceases from his own works comes the joy and peace that he had read about in the Scriptures.

Life takes on new meaning and dimension when each day begins with the knowledge that, **I can do all things through Him who strengthens me** (Phil. 4:13 NAS). That this day, **For to me, to live is Christ . . .** (Phil. 1:21 NAS), and life is now defined as, **. . . Christ in you, the hope of glory** (Col. 1:27 NAS).

However, when temptation comes, the euphoria disappears and, frequently, the believer falls apart. He is confused and wonders how he could be tempted if Christ dwells in him. I have been asked many times, "If Christ is in me, how could I possibly be tempted like this? How could I have the feelings that I do?"

What we must understand is that temptation is not sin. Jesus was **. . . tempted in all things as we are, yet without sin** (Heb. 4:15 NAS). We must dare to take that verse as it stands — Jesus, the sinless, perfect Man, knew temptation in every area and in every way as we do. This should finally convince us that to be tempted is not sin; yet there are countless believers who live in condemnation, just because they feel the call of temptation.

To understand exactly what temptation is will deliver us from constantly struggling with it. We will come to recognize it as a God-chosen method to establish us in our faith.

Before we came to Christ, we were one with the world that **. . . lies in the power of the evil one** (1 John 5:19 NAS), the world that consists of **. . . the lust of the flesh and the lust of the eyes and the boastful pride of life . . .** (1 John 2:16 NAS). Now that we have been **delivered . . . from the domain of darkness, and transferred . . . into the kingdom of His beloved Son** (Col. 1:13 NAS), we are aware of that which we once were a part. While we were in the darkness, we were so accustomed to it, we hardly noticed.

When I lived in New York City, I read about the air pollution. When it was unusually bad, the local news would alert us of the danger. But living inside the city, I was rarely aware of breathing polluted air.

One time, flying into the city, I saw a thick brown cloud hanging over the city, engulfing the buildings. It was the pollution that everyone talked about, but I could only see its filth and ugliness from the outside. So it is, only when we are in Christ, that we know what the world is really like. And in seeing it, we know we are no longer part of it.

Temptation is the strong call to return to the ways of the darkness. It is an appeal to our humanity, our physical appetites, the normal reactions of our emotions and reasonings.

James spells out, step by step, how temptation takes place:

But each one is tempted when he is carried away and enticed by his own lust,

Then when lust has conceived, it gives birth to sin . . . .

James 1:14,15 NAS

The words James uses are important to our understanding of what is taking place. The word *lust* is usually associated with evil; but in actual fact, it simply means "desire or passion" — those desires that are normal to our human flesh. The word *enticed* is a word that belongs to hunters and fishermen. It literally means, "lured by a bait."

When we use words like *lure* and *bait*, we immediately think of being stimulated, excited, drawn toward something. The heart of temptation is that our natural human desires are strongly drawn toward something in the world. James tells us that this is not sin . . . it is only sin when the desire conceives by moving from a reaction to a decision, to deliberately pursuing what is calling.

Someone says something to us that is unkind, unfair or malicious. It is not sin to experience the negative emotional reaction of being hurt, or to have feelings of anger or revenge. This is very normal for a human being.

If I am caught in a traffic snarl, it is not sin to have feelings of impatience or irritation. When there are special guests coming for dinner and everything goes wrong in the kitchen, it is not wrong to feel frustrated and on the edge of tears.

We do not receive a resurrection body when Christ comes to live within us, and we still have all the normal physical appetites common to human beings. We still have hunger, thirst, sex drives, and we are tired after a long day, just as Jesus was. If we have established addictions in our bodies with alcohol or drugs before coming to Christ, it would not be unusual for the body to have flashbacks and send messages to the brain requesting relief as it used to know it.

None of this is sin. I have found so many believers who wear a mask in all of these areas, pretending that they do not even have reactions to life. They are some of the first to burn out, because people cannot live with such unreality.

Gethsemane shows us Jesus in the greatest temptation of His life. He had spoken many times to His disciples of His approaching death and resurrection, and had shown plainly that it was the will of His Father that He should suffer and die. In Gethsemane, as true man, everything in His flesh drew back from such a path, and His temptation was so great that He actually asked His Father if there was another way. But in that, He did not sin.

Sin is when we follow the desire and choose to engage in the forbidden activity. And the fact is, a believer rarely does go that far. Much of the condemnation believers experience is not because they have sinned; they have only been called toward it.

Stand back and see who the believer really is. He is one with Christ.

> . . . **the one who joins himself to the Lord is one spirit with Him . . . .**

> **. . . do you not know that your body is a temple of the Holy Spirit who is in you, whom you have from God, and that you are not your own?**

> **For you have been bought with a price . . . .**

> **1 Corinthians 6:17,19,20** NAS

We are those who have presented ourselves **. . . to God as those alive from the dead, and** *(our)* **members as instruments of righteousness to God** (Rom. 6:13 NAS). We are members of the New Covenant, and the Law of God has been written into our hearts. (Heb. 8:10.)

Joined to Christ at the heart of his being, the believer does not want to sin, he wants to walk in righteousness. Sinners are not tempted! They are in the darkness of their father the devil. Temptation can only take place in those who have exited the world.

When we see a few leaves clinging to a branch in mid-winter, we know they are no longer part of the tree; they died many weeks ago. In the spring, the tree will put off what does not belong to it and put on leaves that are an expression of the new life.

In the same way, temptation brings us to the faith that releases God's life in us, separating us, like the dead leaves dropping off the trees, from the lifestyle of the world.

I saw a snake skin the other day, close to the jagged stump of a tree. I knew what had happened. The snake had grown its annual new skin, and last year's skin became a nuisance, clinging to him without being a part of him. He found a sharp surface and began to scratch where it itched, and he got rid of what was no longer a part of him. It had been him last year, but now it was just an annoying itch. Temptation is the itch that God allows in our life so that we can choose to be who we are, the new creation in Christ.

If we do not understand this, we are prisoners to a morbid fear of temptation. When that is linked with the legalism of the Pharisees, the believer finds himself surrounded by ridiculous laws that forbid many normal, healthy pursuits. All of these fence laws arise out of the minds of Church leaders who are obsessed with temptation and sin. The Scriptures teach that temptation is not to be viewed fearfully, but with a sense of excitement. It is God's chosen method to reveal Christ, again and again, in our lives.

When the strong pull of temptation draws us, if we are going to grow in Christ, we must immediately recognize the real issues with which we are dealing. In two ways, temptation calls us to be who we are not. First of all, the call itself is to do something that, in our hearts, we know is not who we now are in Christ. But the second and real temptation is to forget who we are and become legalistic, trying to overcome it as if we were separated from Jesus.

The legalist appeals to his own will power to obey the Law, whether God's Law or a law that he or his church group has erected. He tells himself, "I mustn't do this; I won't do it . . ." He dedicates himself, hoping to strengthen his will power; he makes promises to God that he will not answer the call to sin. But even while he is promising he will not yield, he is moving towards it!

When he falls into sin, he seeks to handle his condemnation and guilt with rededications and promises that he will not tread that path again. And so, the miserable life drifts on towards burnout.

We do not resist temptation with will power. We resist and overcome it by turning to Christ, our life within. He is recognized as the positive answer to the desires that have been negatively excited. If the call is to impatience, He is our patience. If to hatred and bitterness, He is our love and forgiveness.

It is in this sense that God has chosen temptation as a means to glorify Jesus throughout our lives. Over against the darkness of this world, His light in and by us is clearly seen.

Temptation is not overcome by will power. Even if we are strong enough in ourselves to say "no," we have still failed the test. God did not allow the temptation to show the world the strength of our will power, but as a means to let Christ live mightily through us. The believer never says "no" to temptation, but "yes" to Jesus.

But what happens if we do sin, if we are thrown off balance and forget who we are and find ourselves guilty? Speaking to believers, John said, **If we confess our sins, He is faithful and righteous to forgive us our sins and to cleanse us from all unrighteousness** (1 John 1:9 NAS).

The word *confess* means to say the same thing as. In confessing our sin, we say the same thing about it that God does. We admit that it is indeed sin, but go right on to recognize that it has been dealt with through the blood of Jesus. In doing so, we are agreeing with God that it has been forgiven. We do not slander God by wallowing in guilt and condemnation, but praise Him by going on our way to new adventures of faith.

Hector had been a heavy drug user before he came to know the Lord. But he had had a marvelous conversion, and soon thereafter had been filled with the Spirit. He was reunited with his wife, and she too came to know the Lord.

It wasn't long before he realized that, although he was a new Hector in Christ, he still had strong temptations to return to his old drug habit. One morning at 4 a.m., his wife, Gloria, greatly distressed, called me. Apparently, Hector had been very upset the previous day, and had gone out and had not returned home. She was convinced he had gone to look for a pusher.

In the grey dawn, I went to the area where he had spent his days as an addict. After a few inquiries, I found him in a sleazy pool hall. When I walked in, he was shocked and obviously ashamed that I had found him in that place.

He took me aside and said, "Pastor, please leave me alone! I have let God down, I have let you down and all the brothers and sisters at the church. It's no use, I'm not worth you bothering with anymore."

I didn't listen to his words born out of guilt but, instead, took him to breakfast. He kept saying that God had to be finished with him, now that he had taken drugs again.

I looked him squarely in the eye and said, "Hector, God loved you when you were a junky, and He saved you. Do you think, now that you are His child, He doesn't love you so freely and unconditionally? He still loves you now, even though last night you hurt yourself and your family.

"He loves you in exactly the same way at this moment as He did when you were singing in the Spirit last week. God's love is not dependent on what you do or don't do. He forgives you, take it and thank Him!"

He visibly brightened, and I turned my attention to the question of how he handled temptation when it came, specifically, the temptation to return to drugs. He looked shocked that I would ask the question and assured me that he continually said, "No!"

This was Hector's problem . . . he said "no" to his temptations. He was living by a law that he had written which said something like, "Thou shalt not get high on drugs." With one eye on the law, he set about trying to live up to the image he had of a strong Christian . . . which would be someone who was not tempted by drugs.

When temptation came, he was thrown into guilt that he was so weak as to have such feelings . . . so, he set his will to resist. Wherever there is law, there also is obsession with the sin it forbids; and with that, a hundred desires to experience the sin are aroused . . . as Hector had so miserably discovered.

"Hector," I said, "You must understand that faith never says 'no' to temptation — it says 'yes' to Jesus!" I went on to explain, that the old Hector had been nailed to the cross with Jesus, and that now the Spirit of Jesus lived within him. Life was not a matter of Hector trying to be good, but admitting he never could be good!

Once this was understood, he would never think that Christianity was a matter of adjusting behavior, but, rather, of letting Christ live through him in His strength and power. Faith is not collecting all my will power into a mighty "No!" . . . it is a recognition at the point of my weakness that, even though I do not feel it, Christ is my strength.

Hector seemed to understand and returned to being his usual happy person around the church. Some months later, pressures again developed in his life, and he began to think how getting high for a night would alleviate some of his anxieties. He began to say "No!" but over the next weeks his resistance became weaker and weaker.

Finally, one day as he left for work, he had all but decided to go to a drug dealer and get high. He assured himself that it would be only once. At the same time, what little resistance was left was screaming "No!" as loudly as it could. As he came closer to where he could buy the drugs, he was crying out inside, "Please God, help me!"

Somewhere deep within, he remembered the conversation we had had those months before. "This desire for drugs is not the real me. This Hector died with Christ and I am now risen with Him, and He is my life. And I am trying to deal with this as if He was not inside me. Lord Jesus, I don't want to get high, but I am weak; You take over and live Your victory through me."

In that moment, Hector realized that he was a branch in the vine, and the life was there for him. Faith united with Christ his life. In that moment, Hector became the man he really was in Christ. The Spirit of the Lord came on him, and he walked on his way, praising God. That was many years ago, and he has never been seriously tempted to return to drugs since then.

Chapter 11

A CLASSIC CASE

OF BURNOUT

Thousands of believers are burning out daily because they are expecting things from God that the Gospel does not promise.

Asaph was a man of God in the days of David the king, a writer of a number of psalms and a pioneer, under David, in leading Israel in the joyous worship of God at Mount Zion.

He was born into the priestly tribe of Levi which meant that his destiny was to minister in the presence of God throughout his life. At the time of his birth, due to the apostacy of Saul, the reigning king, interest in spiritual things was at an all-time low.

When David became king, he led the people in a spiritual revival, bringing the Ark of the Covenant back to Jerusalem. It was placed within the walls on Mount Zion; and in the tent where it was housed, uninhibited praise and worship to God took place.

The prayers of hundreds of godly Israelites, who had interceded during the dark days of Saul, had been answered beyond their wildest dreams. David was the instrument in God's hand to bring about a renewal such as had never been seen before. It reminded those who knew the Scriptures of the days of Moses, when Miriam led the whole nation in singing and dancing in worship to God on the banks of the Red Sea.

There was a consciousness of God's presence that demanded the singing of praise and clapping for joy at the magnificence of God. King David himself uninhibitedly danced in worship before the Lord.

This is when we meet Asaph for the first time. He is suddenly catapulted from obscurity into prominence by being chosen to lead the music of praise that escorted the ark on its journey to Jerusalem.

Then David spoke to the chiefs of the Levites to appoint their relatives the singers, with instruments of music, harps, lyres, loud-sounding cymbals, to raise sounds of joy.

So the Levites appointed Heman . . . Asaph . . . and . . . Ethan . . . .

1 Chronicles 15:16,17 NAS

For the leaders to have been aware of his musical ability, Asaph must have had a reputation similar to David's. Years before, as an obscure shepherd boy, David's ability to worship God with his harp was known even in the court.

Immediately after this, David appointed him to the permanent position of leading the worship before the Ark of the Covenant.

. . . as ministers before the ark of the Lord, even to celebrate and to thank and praise the Lord God of Israel:

Asaph the chief . . . with musical instruments, harps, lyres; also Asaph played loud-sounding cymbals . . . .

. . . David first assigned Asaph and his relatives to give thanks to the Lord . . . .

So he left Asaph . . . to minister before the ark continually, as every day's work required.

1 Chronicles 16:4,5,7,37 NAS

Asaph was undoubtedly a man of great spiritual gifts and potential, and was anointed by the Spirit to lead the people in worship. Over the years, he was to write a number of psalms and, years after his death, he would be referred to with the prophetical title of "seer." (2 Chron. 29:30.)

But in those early days after being brought out of obscurity, he was in a dangerous position. He had the heady honor of having his name linked with David's as the psalmist of Israel. By reason of his position, he had a reputation which exceeded his experience.

The uninhibited worship of God involved every physical and emotional sense. The vast choirs and orchestras moved the soul Godward, and there were moments when time and space seemed to be swallowed up by eternity. But the thrill of God's presence cannot be confused with the experience of knowing Him in covenant relationship. God ordained the choirs and the music, but not as a substitute for knowing Him . . . they were meant to be an expression of a relationship with Him.

Praise is not a heavenly drug to deaden the pain of life. It is because we know God that, in the midst of the hurts of life, we can praise Him. Our relationship with God is primarily a faith response, which is often contrary to appearances and feelings. Our life is founded upon Who God is, not upon how we may feel about Him today.

Asaph, King David's associate, the man who led the nation in worship at the peak of its spiritual life, burned out. He became an exhausted man who ministered in the realm of the Spirit. Busy every day in organizing the worship of God, his foundations began to crumble.

It is significant that the Holy Spirit records the testimony he gave in Psalm 73 of how he failed and recovered. He is proof that no one is beyond burning out . . . and he's also the hope that we can move from spiritual exhaustion into the true exhilaration of faith.

Because Asaph carefully documented what led him to his days of spiritual emptiness, the psalm is a vital key to understanding spiritual burnout. He also told us what it was that brought him out — and gave him the rich ministry for which we know him.

He traced the beginning of his problem to the day he began to look at the affluent lifestyle of his unbelieving neighbors. They were materially prosperous and didn't seem to have a care in the world.

Asaph had been raised under the Law of Moses and, although he had been touched by the grace of God under the influence of David and certainly moved in the dimension of the Spirit, he still clung to the old principles of the Law. He believed that his faith, his dedication to God and his work earned him God's material blessing. The covenant was a formula for prosperity and a life of ease.

This is always dangerous because it equates spirituality with possessions and freedom from opposition in life. It was the leaven of the Pharisee before its time, which said, "Because I have done thus and so, then God should give me material blessings." It is the same spirit that we have seen in the elder brother, "Surely you should reward me for all of my service to you!"

The issue here is not whether God blesses His people with material things. He does, but the material things are the postscript to the covenant that has brought us into a dynamic relationship with Him.

This means that the believer has an entirely different attitude toward wealth and possessions than the unbeliever. The unbeliever amasses wealth and gathers possessions as his security against the future, to have power over others and for the aura of importance that it gives him.

The believer knows that God has become to him a security money could never provide, and has given him a new self-image in Christ . . . one of all the honor and glory the human spirit has ever craved. More than that, linked with God Who is love, he now delights to give even as he has been given, and so his life becomes a flowing river of giving, receiving and giving again.

With Asaph, the material possessions and a life free from difficulty had become the issue. The postscript had become the letter! The results of the covenant relationship had overshadowed the relationship itself.

That was when he began to look at his more affluent neighbors, looking at their godless lives and comparing them with his dedication and service to God. "Surely, I deserve to be blessed with no problems and wealth in abundance. Why do they have more than I do?"

He spent hours thinking along these lines, watching how they lived, their attitudes toward God and their ungodly influence on those around them. When he finally began to talk about his feelings, he was envious — the very sight of the wicked disgusted him. He poured out his description of them in angry detail.

> . . . so their pride sparkles like a jeweled necklace, and their clothing is woven of cruelty! These fat cats have everything their heart could ever wish for! They scoff at God and threaten his people. How proudly they speak! They boast against the very heavens, and their words strut through the earth.
>
> And so God's people are dismayed and confused, and drink it all in. "Does God realize what is going on?" they ask. "Look at these men of arrogance; they never have to lift a finger — theirs is a life of ease; and all the time their riches multiply."
>
> **Psalm 73:6-12** TLB

As he meditated on the wicked and the growing conviction that God had treated him unfairly, Asaph began to exaggerate the pleasant life of the unbeliever. By believing the lie, he made his complaints sound right in his own ears.

> For I was envious of the arrogant,
> As I saw the prosperity of the wicked.
> For there are no pains in their death;
> And their body is fat.

They are not in trouble as other men;
Nor are they plagued like mankind . . .
Behold these are the wicked;
And always at ease, they have increased in wealth.

Psalm 73:3-5,12 NAS

By making general and universal statements about the carefree life of the wicked, "No pains in their death . . . . not in trouble as other men . . . nor are they plagued like mankind," Asaph avoids facing the foolishness of the lie that he has chosen to believe.

His life experience had fallen short of what he had been given to believe the Gospel promised. Every day on Mount Zion, he had led the people in singing that God was good and great, the Lord over all the earth.

Looking at what he now perceived as all the facts, he felt that injustice and unfairness reigned . . . and God had vacated His throne. He described himself by saying, **. . . my heart was embittered, and I was pierced within** (Ps. 73:21 NAS).

The word *embittered* describes an angry state of mind, resentment against God for letting things be the way they are. It is accompanied by amnesia concerning all the blessings God has showered in the past. It spills over in angry words, ill will directed at people in general.

Asaph began to exhibit classic symptoms of a burned-out believer. His anger against God, Who he now is certain has let him down and failed in covenant responsibility, expressed itself in cynical remarks.

Surely in vain I have kept my heart pure,
And washed my hands in innocence;
For I have been stricken all day long,
And chastened every morning.

Psalm 73:13,14 NAS

Bitterly, he reviewed his dedication to God, his walk in faith; he asked if there was any point to it. He thought of all he had done . . . led a nation in worship, wrote psalms that would be sung for generations . . . his only reward was to have his days filled with trouble.

His memory was so filtered through his self-pity, he only remembered the bad things and the negatives of his life. He used the term *chastened*, which was used in Scripture to describe God's action. He was saying, "You look after those who laugh in Your face, You let them prosper; but me, Your covenant child, You beat me up every day!"

Mixed with bitterness and jealousy, his questions went around and around in his mind, and always returned to his problem with God.

He was a covenant man! "I thought You could do better than this for one of Your covenant children. How can God be true to His Word, in the light of all that I see? How is it that I don't have all the possessions I want? Why should they have it all? I'm a believer, I should have a life without pain or hurt. God hasn't kept His covenant with me."

He described his experience at that point by saying, **. . . my feet came close to stumbling; my steps had almost slipped** (Ps. 73:2 NAS). Once he began to entertain the distortions of truth, he felt his feet slipping from under him as though he were a man walking on ice. He was about to crash.

With an apparently honorable motive, he found himself withdrawing from his friends. He said, **If I had said, "I will speak thus," Behold I should have betrayed the generation of Thy children** (Ps. 73:15 NAS).

He was really saying, "It looks as if I am going to walk away from everything I have believed, but I don't want to influence others by sharing my doubts with them. Because of my position I have enormous influence wherever people worship God . . . so I will keep my feelings to myself and resign as quietly as possible."

He felt like a hypocrite as he stood before everyone, leading in praise that he did not feel. When anyone greeted him, he responded in the usual way, "Praise the Lord." Inside he said,

"What's the use of going on?" As soon as his work was done in leading the orchestra and choirs, he slipped out by the back door, not wanting to speak with anyone.

However honorable it may have been not to speak with immature believers, he could have discussed the matter with Heman and Ethan, his associates in ministry, and received their counsel and prayer. The classic symptom of burnout is to run away from people and be alone.

But Asaph is in such quicksand that he cannot privately think himself out of it. **When I pondered to understand this, it was troublesome in my sight** (Ps. 73:16 NAS). The words in the original give the idea that, "Trying to understand what was going on was too great an effort for me." Like a man freezing to death, all he wanted to do was lie down and go into an endless sleep.

When he summed up what had happened, Asaph said his heart and flesh had failed. He had burned out and now, faint and exhausted, he had nothing left from which to draw.

Finally, he discerned that his negative attitude was more than him just having a bad day. He described himself as being *bitten*, using a word that is often used in Hebrew to describe being bitten by a snake. He recognized that he had opened himself to be bitten by the father of lies.

He then recalled how he came out of the terrible pit that was sucking him down. He was at the point where he could not be bothered to even try to get out, and he stayed there **until I came into the sanctuary of God . . .** (Ps. 73:17 NAS).

When he said "into the sanctuary," he did not mean the physical structure. To tell a burned out person to go to church will not help very much . . . he perceives that it was the Church which sucked the life out of him! Asaph was in the physical structure called the sanctuary every day of his life, and for the last months it had been the place of his greatest turmoil . . . where he felt the biggest hypocrite.

"The sanctuary," in the Old Testament was the place where God had chosen to make His presence known. The expression *Mount Zion*, the hill inside Jerusalem where the Ark of God was housed, came to be synonymous with the concept of God dwelling with men.

When Asaph came into that place (as he did every day of his life to perform his priestly duties), he became aware of the Person Who filled the sanctuary. He came not to a building, but to the Person the building was all about. He came to the Answer Himself, rather than to a book of formulas and answers.

God's presence gave him an understanding, a perspective on life that he had never had before. If he had, he would not have burned out.

Primarily, it was not his emotions that were helped; it was his mind, his understanding of what was going on. The spiritually exhausted person needs more than the singing of a few inspirational worship songs — they will only momentarily make him feel good. He needs a completely new perspective on the way he thinks about life. When that happens, the inspiration will last a lifetime.

Asaph didn't learn anything that was really new — he came to understand the word he already had that was now made alive and applied by the Spirit. He moved from looking for formulas, answers and keys to being as successful and happy as the wicked, to a relationship with the Father that is the heart of faith.

It was here that he looked back and described himself in the way we have been analyzing. As he told it, it was a repentance, a changing of his mind about the conclusions that had been made in bitterness and self-pity.

He recollected that he had acted more like a beast than a covenant child of God. **Then I was senseless and ignorant; I was like a beast before Thee** (Ps. 73:22 NAS). A beast acts only on the data presented by its senses. Asaph was presently reacting to life, instead of acting within it in the light of all he knew of God.

113

As he considered where he had been and what he had begun to believe, he burst forth with the sudden realization, **Nevertheless I am continually with Thee; Thou hast taken hold of my right hand** (Ps. 73:23 NAS). He realized that, through all his bitter meandering, God had never left him, but had continued in His love for him . . . and had actually been holding him all through it.

Religion is scandalized by such an idea. To have God's presence and His hand guiding, one has to be worthy. A man raging against God while leading worship on Mount Zion is not only not worthy, he is a hypocrite as well! But God does not leave us when, exhausted from trying to explain life with our own limited wisdom, we fall.

One time, I was hitchhiking through the wild countryside of Ireland. The farmer, who picked me up in his old truck, was a local resident. He said he knew a short-cut to a major highway that would take me closer to my destination, and turned his ancient vehicle off the main road onto a muddy cart track. A hundred yards off the road, we sank into thick mud.

I got out and tried to push, but it was stuck fast. I was in a hurry and, although I felt sorry for the farmer, I had to be on my way. Wishing him well, I returned to the highway to look for another lift.

On another occasion, I was driving with a friend and, under similar circumstances, we became stuck. This time, I didn't go on my way; I was committed to reach the destination with my friend and stayed until we were able to pull the truck out.

God is not a hitchhiker! He doesn't leave us when we get off on a side road and stupidly get stuck in the mud. He is committed to never leave us or forsake us. The father had continued to love the prodigal son while he was in the far country, illustrating a love that does not depend on the performance of the one who is loved.

It is an amazing thing that many believe God loves us unconditionally while we are sinners; but as soon as we enter the family, His love is conditioned on our performance. We can accept that He loves unworthy people, until we come to Christ, and then we must continually make ourselves worthy to receive His blessing.

What Asaph discovered in his meeting with God in the sanctuary was that true prosperity begins in relationship with God. The things that he had envied and coveted in his neighbors would all pass away, in this life and certainly in the one to come. But the joy that God gives cannot pass away because it flows from Him, not from things.

Looking ahead, Asaph realized that there would be many times when he would again face areas that could drain him . . . but now he possessed the answer. His relationship with God, and his knowledge of living in union with Him, would carry him triumphantly through whatever the unknown future held.

> **Whom have I in heaven but Thee?**
> **And besides Thee, I desire nothing on earth.**
>
> **My flesh and my heart may fail,**
> **But God is the strength of my heart and my portion forever.**
>
> **Psalm 73:25,26 NAS**

Chapter 12

FAITH —

THE JOY OF THE LORD

Asaph's real problem was in his expectancy of God. There are some things that God has never promised and that He will not do. If we are expecting Him to do what He has not promised to do, sooner or later, we are going to burn out.

Asaph was looking for happiness. In the sense of perfect circumstances, God does not give His children happiness. In fact, He delivers us from both happiness and unhappiness!

The word *happy* comes from the old English word *hap* which Webster defines as "that which comes suddenly or unexpectedly; chance; fortune; accident; casual event." Thus, *hap* means "luck, fate or chance." It is a word created by man outside of God's covenant to describe life as he perceives it. Man sees the events of his life as chaotic with no one in control; therefore, events, people *"hap"* upon him. All is a matter of luck, chance or impersonal fate.

In some parts of the world, people believe their life is controlled by cruel, evil spirits and, therefore, see the chaos of life as a series of *"haps"* thrown in their path by demons.

Think of how the average man meanders through life. Sometimes the *"haps"* drop things in his lap that he likes. He feels he is being treated as he deserves . . . people are giving the respect he feels is due him, his wife is in a good mood and the children get straight As. His favorite football team is winning and the sun shines every day. The *"haps"* make him feel good and give him a sense of well being. He calls his relationship to that configuration of *"haps", hap*piness!

However, much of the time man does not like the *"haps"* or *hap*penings of life that are in his path. People do not do what he wants them to do; it seems that the wrong people are in control. He feels that he is not appreciated and, sometimes, rejected; people hurt him with their words and actions. There are days filled with anxiety, worry and fear. And it rains on the Fourth of July picnic. On all those days, he wishes that all the *"haps"* that have come his way would "un-*hap.*" When those days begin to pile up, he calls himself un-*hap*py.

Man looks for ways to escape from his "un*haps,*" trying to somehow block them from his mind and live in the fantasy of happiness. He doesn't like the world the way it is, he is bored and unhappy, so he seeks a way to escape into a euphoria that will make him momentarily believe that everything is as he wants it.

This is behind all drug addiction from valium to cocaine; it is the philosophy behind the "Happy Hour" at the bar. It is part of the reason millions are riveted every afternoon to soap operas.

Happiness has the appearance of peace, but it is a false harmony which hangs on the fragile thread of everyone and everything fitting into one's plans today. That pseudo peace and happiness is like the spider's web in the hedgerow on a summer morning. It glistens with a million dew drops and has the appearance of a queen's tiara. But by mid-morning, the dew has evaporated and some animal has shattered the fragile threads.

Even in laughter the heart may be in pain, and the end of joy may be grief (Prov. 14:13 NAS). **For as the crackling of thorn bushes under the pot, so is the laughter of the fool, and this too is futility** (Eccl. 7:6 NAS). If a person's peace and happiness depends on people acting as he wants them to, he will spend most of his life in unhappiness.

The Gospel is not a formula whereby the believer is guaranteed that life will align with his idea of the way he believes it should be. Faith is not an inner power that can make all the *"haps"* line up to make the believer *happy*.

As we have noted, Jesus came to deliver us from happiness (a sense of well-being based on outward circumstances). In so doing, He delivered us from unhappiness. We are no longer slaves to happenings or to happiness. Delivered from unhappiness, we do not have the need to escape, but are able to see and face life as it really is.

If a believer has been led to think that God is going to make him happy by causing people and the events of life to fit into his plans, he is on the verge of spiritual burnout.

Faith is not a power that controls God. It cannot order the events of life into a pattern of personal happiness. But true faith introduces us to a dimension that only believers know. There are very few happy people in the Bible, but we do not find unhappy believers either.

The Bible is full of men and women who, because of their faith, are the object of the world's hatred. They are betrayed by their best friends, surrounded by people who make it difficult for them to practice their faith, tempted by the devil and pressured by the world to conform to its standards. And added to this, they share, with all men, life in a fallen world with all its natural ills. Hardly what one would call a picture of happiness!

Yet these people have lives full of laughter. We find them praising God to the point of dancing, clapping and spinning around in delight. And they do all of this while negative things are taking

119

place. These people are not in bondage to what is happening to them, and so they are not slaves to happiness or unhappiness.

Faith has brought the believer to a new dimension of living that does not depend on the events and people around us. It has brought us to realize our union with the Spirit of Christ, and from that comes **. . . the fruit of the Spirit . . . joy . . .** (Gal. 5:22 NAS).

This spiritual vigor that energizes the believer is elsewhere called **. . . joy in the Holy Spirit** (Rom. 14:17 NAS) and **". . . the joy of the Lord . . ."** (Neh. 8:10 NAS). Isaiah, looking forward to the days of the New Covenant, said:

> **And the ransomed of the Lord will return,**
> **And come with joyful shouting to Zion,**
> **With everlasting joy upon their heads.**
> **They will find gladness and joy,**
> **And sorrow and sighing will flee away.**

Isaiah 35:10 NAS

The angel announced to the shepherds in the Bethlehem fields, **. . . "Do not be afraid; for behold, I bring you good news of a great joy which shall be for all the people"** (Luke 2:10 NAS).

"Everlasting joy" is uniquely God's joy. *Everlasting* is a term that describes God Who alone is unbeginning and unending. *Everlasting* is before and after time and is, therefore, not related to the happenings of time. Events belong to time; *everlasting* belongs to God.

The joy of the Lord, everlasting joy, is that joy that He has in Himself. God is infinitely satisfied with Himself. He is the perfect One, and there is nothing that can be added to or subtracted from Him. The joy of God is that He is Who He is!

Consider the revelation God has given us of Himself. The very fact that He has revealed Himself shows us His heart: He is love. He could have left us in our darkness, but He chose to come and enlighten us and call us into fellowship with Himself. Love is not something that He has, but it is His essence, the way

He is. Because of this, He has acted toward us in grace, coming to us and making covenant with us.

In all that He is, He is love, seeking our highest good at His own expense. His almighty power in creation and resurrection has worked for us. He knows us completely and loves us completely. His wisdom has planned the perfect end, that we should be the object of His love eternally. And in all this, He is unchanging . . . never better, never worse . . . for He is the infinitely complete One.

Can we imagine a God Who was not love? Without God having revealed Himself to us, man would never have thought of the Creator as being love. We would have imagined Him as almighty, distant, the ultimate dictator. Man's religions, that have arisen out of his human wisdom, have thought God to be cruel or, at best, a frivolous being, teasing and mocking mankind.

Can we imagine a God Who knows us completely and is determined to hurt us . . . a God from Whom we can never escape, Who delights to harm us . . . an almighty power set on destruction . . . a God Who covenanted to curse us? The wonder of the revelation that love made to man is that God is love!

He has focused Himself in Christ Jesus, the Word, God with us, revealing to us Who He is. The God Whose eternal joy is in His satisfaction with Himself, has announced that His joy and delight find focus in Jesus. **. . . and behold, a voice out of the heavens, saying, "This is My beloved Son, in whom I am well pleased"** (Matt. 3:17 NAS).

Revelation 5:12 (NAS) sums it up this way,
. . . "Worthy is the Lamb that was slain to receive power and riches and wisdom and might and honor and glory and blessing."

And He delights in His people; God likes us and sings for joy over us! **"The Lord your God . . . He will exult over you with joy . . . He will rejoice over you with shouts of joy"** (Zeph. 3:17 NAS).

Because of the perfection of God's purpose, nothing man can do will ultimately upset it. When man rises to dethrone Him, He

121

laughs out of the joy He has in His perfect plan of love . . . and the foolishness of man to even try to destroy it.

> **Why are the nations in an uproar,**
> **And the peoples devising a vain thing?**
>
> **The kings of the earth take their stand,**
> **And the rulers take counsel together**
> **Against the Lord and against His Anointed:**
>
> **"Let us tear their fetters apart,**
> **And cast away their cords from us!"**
>
> **He who sits in the heavens laughs,**
> **The Lord scoffs at them.**
>
> **Psalm 2:1-4 NAS**

As believers, we have been brought into union with God in Christ. In Christ, the joy and satisfaction that God has in Himself dwells in us. The Holy Spirit has opened our eyes and caused us to see and believe the love that God has for us; and when faith rests in that, the result is **. . . the fruit of the Spirit . . . joy . . . .**

The events of life sometimes are not the way the believer wants them to be, sometimes people hurt him and the devil hurls his worst; but in all of this, he rejoices.

Faith does not look at life's events, but sees through what is happening to God in Christ and affirms that He is good and, in every detail of life, is triumphantly working out His perfect and wise plan — whatever appearances might look like.

It is in faith's response and rest in the Lordship of Jesus over all of life that His strength is released into the believer, and the expression of that is joy. **". . . the joy of the Lord is your strength"** (Neh. 8:10 NAS).

Years ago, I stood with my three-year-old daughter, enjoying the warm sun on our heads. Suddenly, dark clouds appeared on the horizon and raced across the sky towards us. Within minutes, an eerie twilight engulfed us, lit by lightning that flashed between the clouds.

My little girl clutched my hand and trembled, "Daddy, the sun has died!"

"No" I told her, "it's still there, shining just the same as it was five minutes ago. We just can't see it right now."

Then the rain began. There was no shelter that we could reach, and so we stood huddled as the rain lashed its fury, soaking us to the skin in seconds. "Daddy, I'm afraid," the little voice said between the thunder claps.

"Don't worry," I said, "the sun is still shining and we'll see it in a minute."

Within ten minutes, the dark moments of the thunder shower had swept on across the plain. Suddenly, all was still and the sun was beating down on our heads. As the steam rose from our clothes, my little girl laughed and said, "You were right, Daddy, the sun never died!"

When all the powers of darkness hurl themselves against us, when people are hurting us and nothing seems to be going right, faith looks through the darkness and says, "He is, and His promises are true. He is in control, He is wise, He is good and He loves me."

It is in this affirmation of faith that the joy of the Lord rises in our hearts, and our relationship with God is established. This is expressed in our lips and lives as we begin to praise and worship God for being the kind of God He is. The believer knows that the problems of life have not interrupted the plans and goals of the One Who is love. He is wise, good and faithful to His Covenant Word.

This joy is always in the heart of the believer, but it is seen to be supernatural when the onslaught of trouble is at its worst. Habakkuk looked at approaching problems and shouted his joy of faith.

> **Though the fig tree should not blossom,**
> **And there be no fruit on the vines,**
> **Though the yield of the olives should fail,**
> **And the fields produce no food,**

Though the flock should be cut off from the fold,
And there be no cattle in the stalls,

Yet I will exult in the Lord,
I will rejoice in the God of my salvation.

Habakkuk 3:17,18 NAS

Praise is faith in action, expressing its heart. Faith looks through the cloud and the rain, and sees the sun still shining. Even though feeling the hurts of life, faith unites with God and rejoices in Him and the joy of the Lord is his strength. (Neh. 8:10.)

It is this joyous response of faith to God Himself that is the victory over the enemy and the problems that surround us. All that follows arises out of this triumphant joy of faith.

Satan's intent is always to make us curse God in the face of every difficulty, to make us walk away bitter. Concerning Job, the sneer of the devil was, "Does Job serve You for nothing? You are nothing more than his slave. If trouble ever comes, he is finished with You."

The difficult time is the testing of our faith. When all the evidence suggests that He isn't there, faith sees through the circumstance and rejoices in God. But that is not the end. If it were, then this position would only be a variation on fatalism.

The believer has submitted to God and has declared, "I believe You, regardless of what I am seeing!" He is now in a position to bring about God's will in the situation. He can say to Christ, Who is his life, "What shall we do with this? How are You going to be glorified in it?"

After Habakkuk, in the face of approaching disaster, had shouted his joyous faith in God, he realized his union with Him. God could now achieve His purpose through him, and overcome the enemy. Habakkuk ended his affirmation of faith in God with the words: **The Lord God is my strength, and He has made my feet like hinds' feet, and makes me to walk on my high places** (Hab. 3:19 NAS). *The Amplified Bible* translates it, **The Lord God is my strength, and personal bravery and my invincible army . . . .**

He could now face all the problems with God-given boldness. God overcoming by him. Faith could now speak with authority, resisting the devil, and be the manifestation of the resurrection life of Jesus among men.

It is the rejoicing of praise that prepares the way for God's will to be done through us. The faith that offers praise to God is in the position to understand exactly what must be said and done to bring about God's will in any situation.

"He who offers a sacrifice of thanksgiving honors Me; and to him who orders his way aright I shall show the salvation of God" (Ps. 50:23 NAS). *The Emphasized Bible* translates this verse, **He that sacrificeth a thank offering will glorify Me — and will prepare a way by which I may show him the salvation of God.**

In the release of praise in the face of difficulty and confusion, we have a way, a road prepared, along which we may walk into the salvation or deliverance that God has prepared for us.

Consider this parable: imagine the Christian life as taking place on the side of a mountain. There are various camps of believers all over the slopes, each group discussing the biggest problem to anyone who lives on the mountain.

At regular intervals, rocks of all shapes and sizes roll down on the camps. The discussion which dominates all of the camp meetings is, "Where do the rocks come from, who is rolling them down on us, and what do we do with them?"

Some believers look at the approaching rock and whimper with fear. They are very unhappy and want the rocks to change course, evaporate, anything so long as they go away. At the prayer meeting, these frightened believers beg everyone to pray for them because the evil rock-throwers are attacking again. "Pray that the rocks will go away," they beg.

These believers are candidates for burnout. They have an expectancy of God that is not true and, therefore, will never be realized. Their concept of the Gospel is that Jesus will remove all the rocks that roll down the mountain; their definition of peace is the absence of rocks from the horizon.

Another believer, who has been influenced by Greek thought more than by the Scriptures, looks at the rocks and sighs, "This is my cross to bear, I will accept it patiently!" His testimony to the other people on the mountain is that His God loves him so much that, on a regular basis, He throws rocks at him. He is the fatalist disguised as a holy person. His whole philosophy is that what is to be, will be.

There are congregations in every city who live crushed by the rocks that roll down the mountain. They sincerely believe that God wants it this way. Their concept of God is similar to the elder brother's image of his father, so there is no Good News that faith can awaken.

These believers have no joy and very little happiness either. It is difficult to get excited about a God Who throws rocks at His children! They live in a state of spiritual exhaustion, struggling to survive in a world of falling rocks and, at the same time, believe that God loves them.

Another believer, although closer to the truth, is also heading for burnout due to the way he handles life. He mocks the fatalist, "You must be crazy to think that God throws rocks at people He loves! I don't believe God wants this rock to fall on me."

The way he understands faith is that he can make the mountain the way he wants it . . . and he wants happiness, with no rocks in sight.

If he is an extremist, he might see the rock coming and say to his neighbor, "There is no rock there. Do not even mention rocks around me or my faith will be destroyed." When the rock rolls over him, he refuses to budge in his confession; and when people ask if the rock hurt, he denies that a rock came anywhere near him.

One of his fellow believers in the same camp, but not so extreme, would approach it a little differently. He, too, would say that God did not throw the rock, the evil rock-throwers did. Believing that faith is a power for his personal use, he tries to use it to dissolve the rock, so he rebukes it and declares it a non-rock! When the rock rolls over him, he is shaken.

The other members of his church will say that he didn't have enough faith, and that's why the rock rolled over him. He then feels that God is as embarrassed over his poor performance as his fellow believers are, and he wonders if, perhaps, God has rejected him for his lack of faith.

Wanting his fellow believers to accept him and to continue in his reputation as a man of faith, he might hide from them the fact that a rock has just hit him. When he does this, he begins the lonely road of mask-wearing, which is one of the first symptoms of approaching spiritual burnout.

When the process continues to be repeated, he is certainly going to burn out. His burnout will be more devastating than that of his stoic friend down the street. In that church they don't expect anything, and actually thank God when they get nothing!

This believer thinks his faith can manipulate life around his goals. When it doesn't work, he will eventually become bitter and walk from what he thinks is the Gospel. His complaint will be similar to Asaph's, "I had faith, but God didn't do anything. He let me down."

For all of this man's sincerity, he will burn out because he does not really have faith in God. He equates natural faith with God's faith, and thinks that it is the currency of heaven with which he can purchase happiness. He erroneously believes that, with enough faith in his heart, he can manipulate God to do things his way.

God will not honor this pseudo faith. The Gospel is, first of all, the announcement of covenant relationship; we are called to know God personally.

Our faith, by which He does work in our lives, arises out of that relationship, not from formulas that allegedly make God do as we say.

God would rather let the stone roll over us than be manipulated by us, because He has so much more for us. He desires us to know Him, out of which relationship all the covenant blessings will flow.

The believer, with faith that is born of the Spirit, looks at the rock rolling down the mountain and feels uneasy. He might feel a twinge of fear and wish that it would go away . . . he doesn't like rocks. But he stops himself from following the thoughts of fear and the desire to run. He tells himself that there is more here than a falling rock. He chooses to see all of the facts, which include more than the rock.

He knows that God is in control of the whole mountain, which includes all the rock-throwers and all the rocks. He also knows that Jesus has risen from the dead and has overcome all the rock-throwers. In the light of these facts, his position is that the rock has been allowed in order to show the glory of the Lord Jesus . . . and to show one more time that all rock-throwers are defeated.

Faith never falls apart at the approach of the boulders of life. It is when rocks are rolling that faith shows up the best.

With praise to God, Who owns the mountain, and to Jesus, the Conqueror of the rock-throwers, the believer with faith stands in the path of the rock and embraces it as it comes. With a shout of triumph, he asks, "What shall we do with this, Lord? How are You going to be glorified this time?" This man, in union with his God, is the master of the mountain and cannot burn out.

Chapter 13

FAITH —

THE PEACE OF GOD

Jehoshaphat was one of the great kings of Judah. So that we can see how he handled all the pressures of life, and why it was that he never became spiritually exhausted, one incident from his life is recorded in 2 Chronicles 20. It capsulizes his faith and puts it under a microscope.

His problem began one day when news came that his neighbors, the Ammonites, the Moabites and tribesmen from Edom, had joined together to dethrone him and take over Jerusalem and Judah. They apparently planned on colonizing their conquest, because they had brought all their belongings with them. Obviously, they had no intention of returning to their own lands. Jehoshaphat is faced with an army of ruthless people bent on wiping out him and his people, and taking over their land.

They had not made a frontal attack where Jehoshaphat's border guards would have been able to warn him. They had come around the southern end of the Dead Sea and climbed over an almost sheer precipice so as to come on Jerusalem almost without warning. By the time spies had reported the approach of the enemy, they were only 15 hours marching time from Jerusalem.

The Scriptures tell us that Jehoshaphat was afraid. In his prayer he describes the situation as one of distress. The word that we translate in our Bible as *distress*, could also be translated as "a narrow constricted canyon; a road that crowds."

In Numbers 22:26 (NAS), the word is translated, **. . . a narrow place where there was no way to turn to the right hand or the left.** It means that everything is crushing an individual, he is feeling claustrophobic in his spirit.

Jehoshaphat was feeling all of this. Life was pressing him to the point that he felt there was no way out, no room to turn, and he was afraid. Fear is faith in all the facts that the five senses present; and according to all the evidence he had, the nation would be overrun within 24 hours.

In life, when we face moments like this, there is a variety of ways we might turn. We can take the path that will use the experience to establish us in our relationship with God, or we can take steps that eventually lead to a burned-out life.

Following a path of feelings of guilt and condemnation is causing thousands to burnout today. The guilt feelings are based on the legalistic error that faith is something that man originates, and that great men of God have a lot of it.

If a believer finds himself with fears, then a flashing red light of condemnation comes on and screams at him, "You don't have enough faith! You haven't been reading the Scriptures and praying enough. You have let down your guard."

The situation is now made more distressing: "God is not pleased with me because of my lack of faith. I must rectify the situation." The poor, lonely believer now begins to try to "unthink" his fears. He may try repeating Bible verses like formulas for success; some even try casting out fears. When he feels strong enough, he will try to rebuke the enemy.

Any time we see faith as something we can create from within ourselves, we are ultimately doomed to failure. The feeling of fear is only the reminder that I am the branch and, of myself, can do nothing. I am completely dependent on the God with Whom I am in covenant. The biblical principle is that when I am weak, then I am strong.

This kind of fear is not sin, it is the human reaction to the circumstances presented to me. It is the nudge that reminds me of my helplessness to handle life in my own strength and wisdom. Faith is my reaction to the greater set of facts that my five senses cannot present to me — the facts arising from the knowledge of the God Who loves me, has covenanted with me, and will never leave or forsake me.

Many years later, the prophet Isaiah would find himself in a similar position. He was inside Jerusalem with attacking armies threatening the city. He describes the state of the city, **. . . his people shook as the trees of the forest shake with the wind** (Is. 7:2 NAS). The Lord spoke to the prophet as to how he was to react: "**. . . you are not to fear what they fear or be in dread of it"** (Is. 8:12 NAS).

He was to not to respond to the same set of facts as the people. They were responding to, accepting, and becoming united with the designs of the great army pitched against them. They were having faith in the facts that were presented to them through their five senses. The Lord commanded Isaiah to "fear," that is, to respond to, a different set of facts.

"It is the Lord of hosts whom you should regard as holy.

And He shall be your fear,

and He shall be your dread.

"Then He shall become a sanctuary . . . ."

Isaiah 8:13,14 NAS

This is what Jehoshaphat did. Instead of pursuing the thoughts of fear, he made a definite choice and **. . . turned his attention to seek the Lord . . .** (2 Chron. 20:3 NAS). Here we face the fact that faith is the gift of God, an expression of the fruit of the Spirit. It does not exist in its own strength, but draws its strength directly from the Lord.

Fear is panic in the mind, looking rapidly from one worthless human solution to another. It is possible to think of confessing Scriptures and even prayer as a formula to solve the problems of life. But it's just one more futile attempt to solve life's problems by using God as one would call up a genie.

Exodus 14:10-15 records the panic of the Israelites as the Egyptians bore down on them. One of their solutions was to call on the Lord, for which He rebuked them. It was an activity of the flesh that looked very spiritual.

Seeking the Lord means that we stop and regroup in the light of Who He is, and who we are in our union with Him. In the psalms we meet the word *Selah* which says, "Stop and think calmly about these things."

To seek the Lord is to realize that He is at the true center of our being . . . to realize that we are not what we are feeling, we are a unity with Him. It is turning the attention to the fact that in us, our very life, is the One Who is the fullness of wisdom, love and power.

It is in this truth that faith is awakened. Faith is not conscious of itself, any more than the eye is conscious of itself. It is taken up with the object it sees. Faith is being taken up with the greatness of God.

Jehoshaphat's prayer describes, in slow motion, faith happening. It tells us what his spirit was doing. He did not look at the situation as it was presented to his senses, but he looked through it to the greater truth. He did not deny the events that were taking place 15 hours away; he simply said that there was more to this situation that his ears were hearing.

... **"O Lord, the God of our fathers, art Thou not God in the heavens? And art Thou not ruler over all the kingdoms of the nations? Power and might are in Thy hand so that no one can stand against Thee."**

2 Chronicles 20:6 NAS

In a sense this is not prayer, and it certainly is not petition. This is the expression of the joy of the Lord; it is praise on his lips concerning the greatness and ability of God at that moment. His rhetorical questions are not reminding God of His ability, but a way of praising Him that this is the way He is.

Jehoshaphat looked at the three nations marching toward him — this was fact. He said, "There is a greater fact, the Lord is ruler over all nations. The alliance of the enemies is a very powerful coalition — true, but all power and might are in the hands of the Lord!"

"Didst Thou not, O our God, drive out the inhabitants of this land before Thy people Israel, and give it to the descendants of Abraham Thy friend forever?

"And they lived in it, and have built Thee a sanctuary there for Thy name, saying,

'Should evil come upon us, the sword, or judgment, or pestilence, or famine, we will stand before this house and before Thee (for Thy name is in this house) and cry to Thee in our distress, and Thou wilt hear and deliver us.' "

2 Chronicles 20:7-9 NAS

Having considered the infinite ability of God in this situation, he then contemplates His covenant commitment to those who were of the faith of Abraham and who called upon Him.

He refers to Abraham with the covenant title of "friend." Jehoshaphat represented the believing people who were united to God by covenant blood. He recognized that they were not just any people, they were a people who were the focus of covenant love.

He went on to remember the dedication of the temple in the days of Solomon when he prayed for protection from all enemies. God had answered that prayer by filling the house with His glory.

In these words of praise, Jehoshaphat reminded himself that God still stood by that answer and would protect them, even as He had promised Solomon that He would.

Jehoshaphat appealed to the committed and willing love of God. Seeing God in a situation and choosing to praise Him, faith is awakened. It is a small matter to present his petition at this time.

> **"And now behold, the sons of Ammon and Moab and Mount Seir . . . .**
>
> **". . . are rewarding us, by coming to drive us out from Thy possession which Thou hast given us as an inheritance.**
>
> **"O our God, wilt Thou not judge them? . . . ."**
>
> **2 Chronicles 20:10-12 NAS**

Faith does not deny the presence of the problem, but calmly places the matter into the hands of God. Jehoshaphat finishes the prayer with one of the greatest statements of faith in the Bible:

> **". . . For we are powerless before this great multitude who are coming against us; nor do we know what to do, but our eyes are on Thee."**
>
> **2 Chronicles 20:12 NAS**

He is simply stating that he has no expectancy in his human ability or wisdom. He is unashamedly declaring himself a helpless branch. He is not threatened, guilty or condemned by that position, but takes it as an opportunity to abandon himself to the God of infinite ability and love.

It was in this statement of faith that Jehoshaphat had the victory. The Spirit bore witness to this among the people.

> **". . . 'Do not fear or be dismayed because of this great multitude, for the battle is not yours but God's . . . .**
>
> **'You need not fight in this battle; station yourselves, stand and see the salvation of the Lord on your behalf . . . .' Do not fear or be dismayed; tomorrow go out to face them, for the Lord is with you."**
>
> **2 Chronicles 20:15,17 NAS**

The people responded with loud praise. The matter was done, and they went to bed and slept soundly. During the night their enemy marched on, planning to take Jerusalem with a surprise attack the next day; but Jehoshaphat, knowing that the battle was already won, slept. Faith does not struggle and sweat; it goes to bed thanking God that He will watch over His victory during the night.

The final expression of faith was in the morning when they went to meet the enemy, and Jehoshaphat sent the choir in the front line.

> . . . he appointed those who sang to the Lord and those who praised Him in holy attire, as they went out before the army and said, "Give thanks to the Lord, for His lovingkindness is everlasting."
>
> 2 Chronicles 20:21 NAS

Lovingkindness is a word describing the covenant faithfulness of God, the assurance that He has given that He will never leave or forsake His people. It was as they took this final expression of faith that the victory they already had became manifest.

> And when they began singing and praising, the Lord set ambushes against the sons of Ammon, Moab and Mount Seir . . . so they were routed.
>
> 2 Chronicles 20:22 NAS

The enemy apparently destroyed themselves, leaving all of their possessions in their tents. It took Israel three days to carry all of the wealth back to Jerusalem. They not only had a victory, but came out of it richer in their knowledge of God and also in material things.

There is strong evidence to believe that Psalm 84 was written at this time. Verse 6 of that psalm would suggest that they were to meet the enemy in the Valley of Baca. It is an unknown valley somewhere outside of Jerusalem.

Baca means "tear shrubs; weeping." A literal translation might be "valley of misery." The verse reads: **Passing through the valley of Baca, they make it a spring . . .** (Ps. 84:6 NAS). The believer

135

spoken of here turns a valley of tears into a refreshing well, the sorrows of life become the opportunity to drink deeply of God.

It would appear that this is the valley that was renamed. **. . . Therefore they have named that place "The Valley of Beracah" until today** (2 Chron. 20:26 NAS). *Beracah* in Hebrew means "blessing." Faith in God is the means by which He walks into our lives and turns every tear into triumph and blessing.

The believer, who faces the problems of life with the knowledge of his relationship to God in Christ, cannot burn out — regardless of the problems that face him. He may be distressed and sometimes perplexed, but he lives at the center of the peace of God.

Chapter 14

LIVING IN THE SPIRIT

One November afternoon, I saw the German Shepherd. It had been raining most of the day, and the mist clung to the mountain. The dog was cringing in the woods at the bottom of my garden. Tail between its legs, its sodden, matted coat was clinging to its emaciated body. From where I stood, I could see the dog was shivering from the cold. I began to walk towards it, but it turned and slunk off into the mist.

Many of our neighbors tried to feed the dog, but it cowered, snarling at its benefactors. Finally, the humane society captured it. Some time later, I learned the animal had been repeatedly beaten by a vicious, half-crazed owner until it ran away to wander the countryside, not daring to trust another human being.

In every city, there are many believers who are lonely, shivering in a spiritual cold, cowering from those who want to do them good. They are wounded in their spirits, verbally beaten, in one way or another, by their fellow believers.

They see themselves as worthless before God and are afraid to share their hearts with another human being, in case they would be condemned and rejected again. They are like that German Shepherd . . . alienated, afraid and lonely.

Isaiah perfectly saw the heart of Jesus and what He came to do. He summed up His character and ministry in chapter 42:3 (NAS) of his prophecy: **"A bruised reed He will not break, and a dimly burning wick He will not extinguish . . . ."**

Reeds grow in abundance by the rivers of Israel. Children would sit on the river bank, hollowing them out to make musical pipes. It was a delicate task as the reed could easily be bruised in the making. If bruised, it was useless for making music; and the children would break it and throw it into the river. There were plenty more reeds to work with!

Isaiah said that, when Messiah Jesus would come, **"A bruised reed He will not break . . . ."** He would be characterized as the One Who would not discard those who were bruised in the making.

In Bible days, Israelite homes were lit by little oil lamps. A wick made of flax floated in the oil and gave light to the house. If the oil ran out, the stench of the burning flax was nauseating; embarrassed, the wife would throw it out of the window. She had a box full of wicks and discarding one would make no difference.

But Isaiah said that when Jesus came, **". . . a dimly burning wick He will not extinguish . . . ."** He would not throw out those who were charred by life and only faintly burning. One possible translation of the words *dimly burning* is literally, "burned out."

The Pharisees discarded those who had failed in life; Jesus restored these bruised reeds and made them musical instruments that played His song of grace. He took the smoking remnants of life and made them into His vehicles through whom He would be the Light of the world.

Neil sat in my office. He was a young man in his early thirties who had been advised to talk to me by some of his friends. He sat in the chair opposite me, and I noted his bearing. He was suspicious, ready to run at any moment. I remembered the German Shepherd.

Hesitantly, he told me of marital problems and of the divorce that had recently taken place. He and his wife had had problems that were long standing, but they had been careful to keep them from the public. They had kept the image of the perfect Christian family. Then a year previous, the dead marriage was out in the open, its ugliness for everyone to pick over like vultures around a carcass.

His voice was tinged with anger. "Before I was saved, people used to witness to me. They talked about the love of Jesus, His mercy and grace. They also talked about what the Church was supposed to be like. It sounded too good to be true — an incredible community of people who loved one another and forgave each other . . . just as they had been forgiven by God! They talked about God being in all things, even in the sorrows and mistakes of life."

His lip curled and he said bitterly, "I bought what they said, and it worked more or less. In the areas where it didn't work, we put on a mask and said, 'Praise the Lord.' Then I made the great mistake! I stopped lying and told them the truth about myself and our marriage. I told them that my marriage was a farce and had been dead for years.

"As soon as they knew the truth about us, it became obvious they had never loved us, but rather the image that we had projected of being the right kind of people, doing the right kind of things. Since our divorce, the church has treated both my ex-wife and me like lepers."

Tears welled in his eyes. "Do you know what they said? They said I was a bad influence on the church, and I had let down my witness before the world. If I would not resign, they would have to excommunicate me to maintain their stand for holiness.

"And then," he hesitated before spitting out the words, "they said they would always love me and pray for me!"

His head dropped wearily, and he stared at the carpet. "Both of us were hurting; we knew for years that we had missed the path somewhere. We needed love and acceptance, but all they said was that we were not performing properly, to leave and stop embarrassing them."

He looked up and said hopelessly, "Is this what you call Christianity? Is this love?"

I sighed deeply. It was a far cry from the One of Whom Isaiah had spoken Who would specialize in broken, battered reeds and charred, burned-out flax.

The fellowship that Neil belonged to were themselves burned out, pastored by relatives of the "elder brother" and, tragically, didn't know it. They were proclaiming a hideous distortion of the Gospel, twisting the Scriptures into saying that acceptance with God was based on performance and behavior.

Their message was, if one does good, there is acceptance by God and His Church; but if one is a failure, then there is divine rejection which is endorsed and carried out by His Church.

These people had no comprehension of the agapic love of God. Each one of them was trying to earn his acceptance with God by doing better than the man in the neighboring pew. When a member fails, there is a certain kind of gloating that says, "I am not as other men who make such hideous mistakes." These folks only know one way to deal with an offender — rejection and expulsion! The image must be maintained that we earn our right to God's acceptance by how we act.

The watching world is not surprised at the harsh and vicious treatment the Church metes out to its hurting members. The only Gospel they have heard is that being a Christian is a matter of achieving incredibly good behavior. It follows that those who do not make the grade must be discarded.

Nodding wisely, much of the world congratulates itself one more time that it never got mixed up with the fighting, arguing Church members. Others shake their heads in sorrow, knowing deep inside that God is not like that. Somewhere, there must be a reed-mender and a lighter of burned-out wicks.

Neil was not right either, his anger and bitterness were wrong; but he was desperately lonely and hurting in his spirit, and God's covenant people had treated him like a pariah dog. It's hard to believe God loves us when His people reject us.

There are other shivering, lonely brothers and sisters who have not sinned, but have become victims of power-hungry elders who understand the Church as a dictatorship in the Name of God. These false shepherds define spirituality as mindless obedience to their demands. Many sincere believers have become caught up in such fellowships, believing they would be the pathway to Christian maturity.

After a time, it became obvious to them that they were being asked to act contrary to what they saw in the Scriptures and what the Spirit witnessed in their hearts. They refused to go along with the lifestyle that was being imposed on them by their elders, and were then expelled, labeled unsubmissive and rebellious. Their friends were told to shun these rebels or suffer the same fate by association.

These wounded sheep have nowhere to turn. They feel that those they have trusted as the Voice of God have cut them off from God and His Church. They cringe in the woods at the edge of the Church, afraid to trust another elder or fellowship.

And then, there was Elizabeth. She was raised in an extremely rigid group that understood acceptance by God and spiritual maturity in terms of keeping the rules.

She looked around at the Sunday morning gathering, everyone dressed in their Sunday best, smiling, murmuring words of greeting to each other and punctuating their conversation with discreet, "God is good," "Praise the Lord," and "Hallelujah." However, Elizabeth knew from being in their homes during the week that it was a great farce.

These were lonely, confused and hurting people who were afraid to speak their true feelings to those they called friends. They had been taught that good Christians do not have bad thoughts or feel like giving up in despair at times. So each lonely soul lived behind a mask he thought would make him acceptable and likable to other members of the congregation. For fear of rejection, they did not dare to share the festering wounds behind their masks.

Many years later, Elizabeth told me that she had wanted to stand up and say, "Look, I'm not the good Christian you think I am! I am proud, scream at my kids and, many times, resent my husband. I hate this town and drag myself to services on Sunday, not really wanting to come. I live in constant worry that I can't pay my bills. Now that you know the real me, do you still love me?"

However, instead of saying anything like it, she continued to sit in the loneliness of what many thousands call fellowship . . . a bruised reed sitting with other bruised reeds, all pretending to be singing God's song.

One day, she could take the hypocrisy no longer. She told these people that she wanted a normal social life and an atmosphere in which she could be honest without fear of rejection. Elizabeth wandered for years, afraid of those who called themselves Christians. The great tragedy was she believed that, by leaving what she understood to be the Church, she was leaving God.

When Elizebeth left, all the members praised God that a false believer had been weeded out, saying they would be holier for her departure. They adjusted their masks and assured each other that they would never take the path that she had chosen.

Elizabeth was a battered reed for many years until one day she discovered the grace of God.

The Pharisee has no place in his theology for a failure. That is when the bruised reeds and smoking flaxes feel their desperate loneliness and rejection. They are driven to utter helplessness, but their rejection by the Pharisees, though it hurts so keenly, is really a blessing from God!

If Elizabeth had known the true Gospel, she would have realized that, when she stepped out of that particular fellowship,

God was actually leading her to the rest and joy that is found in trusting the resurrected One, instead of man-made religious rules.

The same holds true for those who have suffered at the hands of religious dictators. The hands that so callously expelled can now be seen as the hands of God in disguise, bringing about the atmosphere where the grace of God can be seen and enjoyed. God has graciously wrenched the bruised reed from the bondage of outward rules to begin to enjoy life in the Spirit.

Are you a bruised reed? Have you been designated a smoking flax by your brothers? What is it you have been expelled from . . . an atmosphere of constantly trying to live by a list of rules that have no roots in Scripture, imposed on you by an eldership that does not know God's grace . . . a climate in which spirituality is gauged by mindless submission and obedience to these elders? You have not been expelled . . . you have been rescued! Look beyond the fury of the Church and all the hurts involved in expulsion from friends and fellowship. God is bringing you to see that the way to walk with Him is not by a list of rules imposed from the outside, but by the inner life and urgings of the Holy Spirit.

What a relief! Although some of God's misguided children have thrown you out as a useless reed and written you off as a burned out, embarrassing flax, God hasn't. He says, "Now you are ready to let Christ be your life."

"But," someone objects, "I have truly sinned and cannot imagine that God would forgive me; I was a Christian when I did it, and I knew better."

David was unquestionably one of God's sheep. His psalms have made him the song of God among men. He had experienced a lot of life and had just entered into his fifties.

His neighbor was Uriah, one of his most loyal and devoted soldiers. They had been friends for many years, all the way back to when both of them had lived in the wilderness when Saul's men sought their lives. In those days and many times since, Uriah had risked his life for David.

While Uriah was away fighting on the front lines, David entered into an adulterous relationship with Bathsheba, Uriah's wife. When David discovered that a child was to be born of the relationship and there was no way to cover it up, he arranged for the murder of his friend. After Uriah's death, there was a week of public mourning, and then David married Bathsheba.

Israel gossiped. David was a reed that no longer made God's music. To those who guessed what had happened, he was an embarrassment, the stench of a smoking flax. But it is God's delight to take bruised reeds and make them into fine-tuned instruments for His orchestra.

For a year, David sat lonely and wounded by his own sin. He expressed how he felt in those days when he later described them in a psalm:

> **. . . my body wasted away**
> **Through my groaning all day long.**
>
> **For day and night Thy hand was heavy upon me;**
> **My vitality was drained away as with the fever heat of summer.**
>
> **Psalm 32:3,4** NAS

Then Nathan the prophet came and confronted David with his sin, the cause of his hurt. At that time, David poured out his heart to God in Psalm 51. Throughout all the verses and stanzas of the psalm, one thing stands out: David is utterly confident that, in spite of everything he has done, God still loves him and is on his side.

There was no pardon under the Law of Moses for adultery or murder, so the Law condemned him without mercy. People gossiped and said that God had cast him off. But David looked beyond all condemnation to God and dared to believe that he was infinitely and eternally loved. He appealed to that love when he prayed:

> **Be gracious to me, O God, according to Thy lovingkindness;**

According to the greatness of Thy compassion blot out my transgressions.

Psalm 51:1 NAS

One of the most amazing verses in that prayer is verse 11: **Do not cast me away from Thy presence, and do not take Thy Holy Spirit from me.** David knew that God had not cast him off and that the Holy Spirit was still with him. Whatever people said, he rested in the God Whose love would not let him go.

Are you wounded and lonely, ridden with true guilt? With everything people are saying about you, it may be difficult to believe, but your first step is to realize that you are loved. You need to understand that you have failed but, having done so, you need to know God says that He accepts you.

Before the grace of God can take our mistakes and turn them into our strengths, there must be a response to Him. That response is repentance and faith.

Repentance is simply changing our minds about ourselves and our actions. We see things God's way. It means that we admit to God that we are wrong and turn helplessly to Him. If we choose the path of sin, refusing to acknowledge it as sin, we cannot expect the redemption of our failures, only a compounding of despair.

Paul spoke scathingly to this in Romans 6:1,2 (NAS):

What shall we say then? Are we to continue in sin that grace might increase?

May it never be! How shall we who died to sin still live in it?

Faith responds to God's love and His pardon that is ours in what Jesus accomplished when He died and rose again. Outside of Christ, there is only despair over failure. The Christian looks at his defeats and mistakes and turns to God's complete forgiveness and the outworking of Christ Who now lives within. Faith dares to say that God makes the dark hole of our lives the foundations of His most beautiful buildings.

I am an organic gardener, which means that I am continually working with the soil in which my vegetables grow. To do this, I collect all of the scraps from the kitchen, any garbage that will decompose, and put it into my compost heap. Over the months, that heap of refuse becomes the richest soil in my garden.

So God takes the embarrassing refuse of our mistakes and, by His grace, turns it into the strongest and richest soil of our lives.

Disregard the condemnation that people heap upon you; instead, believe the pardon that is yours in Christ. God does not condone sin, but it is adding sin to sin to wallow in guilt and condemnation which tramples underfoot the pardon that Jesus has purchased for us. Remind yourself of God's Word: **. . . "What God has cleansed, no longer consider unholy"** (Acts 10:15 NAS).

At this point, let faith take a giant step and realize that in all the circumstances that have led to this moment God has been at work. There is a real devil, but God in His sovereignty works in all things. Faith sees through the circumstances to God's presence and activity in it. It is hard to understand that God is working in the hurt when you are the one hurting . . . but He is!

One of the first things a Pharisee tells a bruised reed is of all the things that might have been if only right decisions had been made. The look on his face tells you that there is no future now . . . not after what you have done. If you do continue on with God, it will be in His secondary and permissive will.

This is the logical conclusion of legalism. If you had kept the rules, all would have been well; the fact that you haven't has left you only with regrets and no hope.

"If only" and "what might have been" do not exist in God's vocabulary. The pulsating *now*, with all its problems and hurts, is the only reality. Christ does not live and express Himself in the wishful world of dreams, but in our present and actual history. Our mistakes and failures do not send Him away! He makes all the negatives in our lives the expression of His positive answer. He does not say, "What if?" He asks, "What now?"

Proverbs describes the fool and sluggard as a man whose eyes are ever on the horizon, never looking at what is now. The wise man, on the other hand, knows what might have been is not, and so embraces life as he immediately finds it.

I know from personal experience what it is to sit on the edge of life's craters and inhale the sulphur of defeats, failures and sin. I have been angry with myself, knowing that I am responsible for my foolish decisions and wrong actions. Above the clamor of my thoughts, I hear myself saying, "If only I had not done thus and so . . ." or, "What might have been today, if I had acted differently."

Everything within me wants to join the inner conversation, to agree and discuss with myself what might have been. Instead, I take myself in hand. The fact is, I have done what I have done, acted as I have acted and said what I have said.

To live in the fantasy world of "if only" will paralyze me in the real world of now. To retreat into the world of "might have been" is to further fester the wounds that my spirit already has.

Wallowing in that fantasy world slanders God's character as well. He knew from before the foundation of the world what we would say and do. He knew that we would be bruised reeds in the making, yet He loved us, knowing it all.

Now that the failure has been actualized in history, He does not stop loving us. To say, "if only," is to place God alongside the finite gods of the pagans that can be surprised by the activity of their worshippers.

The wonder of God's *agape* wisdom is that He takes our mistakes and weaves them into His plan. One of the overlooked verses of Scripture is in the genealogy of Jesus as recorded in Matthew in his first chapter. When we come to the name of Solomon on that list, the Holy Spirit makes special note of the fact that his mother was Bathsheba.

It is as if God is saying, "See I am not thwarted by the sins of My people; rather, I use their mistakes, incorporating them into

147

My plan. Through the worst that David did, I turned it around and made it a vehicle to bring My Son into the world."

The Gospel is not only the message of forgiveness, but also the message of hope that God will turn the worst into the best. It tells us that God is now at work in our situation, as we are, where we are, glorifying His Name. God does not condone sin, but neither does He grind His plans to a halt, whining, "If only he had seen what I was getting at!"

But what about the wail of the Pharisee? Is he right, has our failure or wrong choice excluded us from God's best? What we should be asking is, "Can the infinitely perfect One have anything in His plans but the best?"

There are many routes that lead to the consummation of His plan for us, but all of them are the best because we are dealing with the God Who can only be the best. Nowhere in Scripture is there a mention of a permissive will of God.

Let us suppose I am traveling from Seattle to New York. There is a plane change in Chicago; but due to weather conditions, I miss the connection. I am not doomed to spend the rest of my life in the Chicago airport. There are other flights from Chicago to New York.

I do not sit in the departure lounge wringing my hands and saying, "If only I hadn't missed the flight." Rather, I accept the fact that I have missed it, and set about making arrangements to fly out on the next available flight.

I may have missed meeting the person who would have sat next to me and maybe the meal that might have been served. But there will be someone else to meet on the next flight, and the airline will serve a comparable meal.

When we fail, God does not condemn us to the departure lounge of His second best. Life should not become the despair of dwelling on what might have been. The infinitely wise One has other ways of accomplishing His will and purpose in our lives. Our involvements will be different and the circumstances too, but they will come up to the standard of His good and perfect wisdom.

Chapter 15

SUDDEN BURNOUT

There are times when believers, who walk in faith in the grace and love of God, suddenly burn out. None of the factors that usually lead people to burn out were in their lives, yet suddenly they are too tired to go on. These believers are not like the candle that gradually burns down, sputters and goes out. This candle was burning merrily and, suddenly, the flame is out; and everyone turns and asks, "What happened?"

Elijah was such a person. When we see him at the peak of his career, it is hard not to think of him as some kind of super-believer, one who is in a different class from others. It is interesting that he is the only believer in Scripture that we are cautioned to think of as a very ordinary person. **Elijah was a human being with a nature such as we have — with feelings, affections and constitution as ourselves . . .** (James 5:17 AMP).

We know very little about Elijah. In fact, very few people ever knew anything about him. He came from the wild, lonely hills of Gilead where his only companion was the God of covenant and the words He had committed Himself to keep on behalf of His people.

From his distant mountain retreat, Elijah watched Israel spiritually hijacked by Jezebel, the heathen wife of Ahab, king of Israel. She was from Sidon, a nation to the north of Israel. The marriage had been arranged to bind the two nations closer together.

Jezebel was a princess in the family of the Sidonian king, Ethbaal, who because of his royal blood was also the high priest of the Baal cult. In one form or another, *Baal* (which means "lord" or "master") was worshipped throughout Canaan and north into Tyre and Sidon. The Baal was looked upon as the source of life and fertility; and among an agricultural people, every hill and mountain was dedicated to the Baal idols.

The Baal cult in Sidon was known as *Baal Melkart*. He was seen as the god of fire and power, his symbol a battle ax. His god-wife was Asherah, the source of fertility and all that it took to make crops grow and animals multiply. In a farming community, to worship Baal meant the promise of an abundance of crops and cattle, which in turn meant wealth and power.

With the focus of the religion being on power and fertility, it brought with it an obsession with sex. The temples of Baal and Asherah were served by armies of priests and priestesses, all who were sacred prostitutes to be enjoyed in worshipping the deities.

Baal Melkart was synonymous with every form of sexual immorality and deviation, materialism and greed. And when Jezebel was chosen as a bride for Ahab king of Israel, she determined to hand her husband and his people over as an offering to her god.

When the marriage took place, Israel was at an all-time low in their spiritual life. Jezebel brought evangelists with her who rapidly turned the people away from anything that remained with them of the worship of the covenant God. It was not long before altars to Baal were to be found on every hill and mountain.

Soon after she arrived in Israel, Jezebel was personally supporting 450 prophets of Baal and 400 of Asherah. Ahab was a weak person who had no time for any religion; he indulged his wife in what he considered her hobby, while he gave himself to his horses!

As Elijah surveyed the scene and prayed, the word of the Lord came to him from the ancient covenant book of Deuteronomy. In chapter 28, God had listed all the blessings that would come to His people as they walked in covenant; He had also listed all the curses that would overtake them if they forsook the covenant.

It was revealed to Elijah that the covenant-forsaking Israel was to be visited with one of these curses, and that he was to be the vehicle through whom it should come. The verse that gripped his spirit was:

"And the heaven which is over your head shall be bronze, and the earth which is under you, iron.

"The Lord will make the rain of your land powder and dust; from heaven it shall come down on you until you are destroyed."

Deuteronomy 28:23,24 NAS

When Elijah came down from the mountains of Gilead and walked through the land, there was no indication that Israel had ever worshipped any god but Baal. There was no sign of a believer in the Lord God of Israel in any village he passed through.

Thousands of believers were scattered though the land, but they were hidden from the spies of Jezebel. The fanatical woman quickly put to death any who would not convert to Baal. Already, many had died for their faith.

One key figure in saving the lives of many prophets of the Lord was employed by the queen. Obadiah, who was in charge of all that happened in the palace, had taken a hundred of God's prophets and hidden them in caves and personally made sure they were fed every day . . . probably from the royal kitchen!

Elijah had little time for anyone who was hiding for his life. His name, *Elijah*, meant "the Lord is God." In a society where everyone said, "Baal is God," the very saying of Elijah's name was throwing down the gauntlet, challenging everyone who dared to name another as their god. His attitude was somewhat arrogant:

151

"If they want to hide, then I will confront the idolatrous nation alone."

He went to the palace and stood before Ahab, and announced, ... **"As the Lord, the God of Israel lives, before whom I stand, surely there shall be neither dew nor rain these years, except by my word"** (1 Kings 17:1 NAS).

In speaking to Ahab, he revealed something of the fears that were going to be his downfall at a critical time in his life. Why didn't he confront Jezebel? She was the high priestess of the vile religion that was the cause of the curse. But Ahab did not want to get involved with these matters. It is possible that Jezebel did not get the report of Elijah's visit to the palace for days afterward.

According to the prophet's word, the rains ceased and overhead the sun beat down week and after week. The crops began to wilt and water became a problem. In a land where the people had given themselves to the god who claimed to be in charge of rain, sunshine and crop growing, the nature of this curse is humorous.

Directed daily by the voice of God, Elijah received divine protection at the Brook Cherith where ravens brought him food morning and evening. From there, the Spirit directed him into the land of Sidon, the source of *Baal Melkart;* and in the city of Zarephath, he was miraculously provided for — along with a widow and her son.

After three and a half years of drought throughout the whole area, the word of the Lord came to Elijah, directing him to the next step. The people had lived with the curse which had shown the impotence of Baal to produce rain — and now they must be brought to faith in the living God.

As recorded in Scripture, it would be true to say that Elijah was afraid of nothing and no one. He had come from the mountains to stand fearlessly in an apostate nation; fearlessly, he had spoken the curse to Ahab and lived without fear during the three and a half years of famine . . . confident in God's supply.

He then came to the greatest challenge to date. It demanded a supernatural fearlessness. He was to challenge the whole cult of *Baal Melkart* before the nation. The place was Mount Carmel, a high mountain on the Meditteranean coast, which had become a center of the Baal cult.

Elijah went into Israel and met with Obadiah. He showed a certain contempt for the man who had not declared himself a believer in the palace. The fact that Obadiah had fed the Lord's prophets meant little to Elijah.

The prophet ordered Obadiah to carry a message to Ahab which, in effect, commanded the king to meet with him. Elijah made it plain that he, not Ahab, was in control of the events of the next hours. It is of note that he did not invite Jezebel.

The two men, Elijah, in a hair cloak, and Ahab, in the finery of the palace, met at the place of Elijah's choosing. Elijah gave Ahab his orders: all Israel was to gather at Mount Carmel, along with the 450 prophets of Baal and the 400 priestesses of Asharah.

Ahab despised him but, amazingly, obeyed him! The message was sent out. Jezebel may have been very angry with him for so weakly obeying the prophet. It is significant that she did not attend, nor did the 400 who were under her direct control. Everyone else did.

Elijah stood alone, as he always did. The multitudes of Israel gathered on the mountain, the king on his royal chair, and the prophets of Baal arrayed in their white robes and hats, at home on this mountain where many conventions of the cult took place.

One might ask, "Where are the thousands of believers today?" It was a question that came to Elijah more than once as he surveyed the scene before him. This was not a day to be hiding in a cave, eating food carried secretly from Jezebel's kitchen. It was not a day to be praying behind locked doors.

This was the day to stand up and be counted with Elijah. But that day, Elijah was the sole representative of the covenant God, facing a nation of Baal worshippers and their fanatical priests. In command of the situation, Elijah threw out his challenge:

> **And Elijah came near to all the people, and said, "How long will you hesitate between two opinions? If the Lord is God, follow Him; but if Baal, follow him." But the people did not answer him a word.**
>
> **Then Elijah said to the people, "I alone am left a prophet of the Lord, but Baal's prophets are 450 men.**
>
> **"Now let them give us two oxen; and let them choose one ox for themselves and cut it up, and place it on the wood, but put no fire under it; and I will prepare the other ox, and lay it on the wood, and I will put no fire under it.**
>
> **"Then you call on the name of your god, and I will call on the name of the Lord, and the God who answers by fire, He is God." And all the people answered and said, "That is a good idea."**
>
> **1 Kings 18:21-24 NAS**

By making the challenge the bringing of fire from the sky, Elijah was confronting everything for which *Baal Melkart* stood. He was the god of fire! The god of the life-giving sun! Let him show himself for what he is. In Baal temples, the priests regularly produced fire on the altars by a mechanism within the altars. Here in the open, Elijah calls for a real demonstration of their god.

The Baal priests began their wild dances, whirling and spinning, accompanied by howling and screaming. As the hours went by, they cut themselves with knives until blood flowed freely. Elijah stood by, fearlessly mocking them in a loud voice.

> . . . **"Call out with a loud voice, for he is a god; either he is occupied or gone aside, or is on a journey, or perhaps he is asleep and needs to be awakened."**
>
> **1 Kings 18:27 NAS**

He let them continue until mid-afternoon, the time when the evening sacrifice was being offered to the Lord in His Temple in Jerusalem. He then built the altar to the Lord and placed the sacrifice on it. He ordered barrels of water from the sea below to be poured over the sacrifice — no one would be able to say he had trick fire. His prayer was simple and short; and it was answered immediately with fire that burned up the sacrifice and turned the water to steam.

The multitude of people went wild, screaming, "The Lord, He is God; the Lord, He is God." The prophets tried to escape, but they were captured and Elijah personally executed them according to the justice of the day — for their crime of leading the nation astray and for the multitude of believers they had put to death.

But Elijah was not finished. He went to the top of Mount Carmel and prayed. Six times, he sent his servant to look out across the sea for a sign of rain clouds, but each time the young man saw only the vast blue expanse. The seventh time he came back with the report that there was a cloud like a man's fist.

Elijah knew that his prayer was answered. He tells Ahab, who is enjoying a royal picnic, to quickly return to the palace or he will be caught in the rain storm. The Spirit comes upon Elijah, and he begins to run with such speed that he outruns the speeding chariot of Ahab.

Run with Elijah, feel your hair streaming behind you, the rain on your face! The Lord has proven himself God. He stopped rain, He sent fire, and now He sends rain. The crops will grow, and everyone will give glory to God knowing that Baal had nothing to do with it. Your mind leaps ahead as you race toward Jezreel!

You know that all Israel will tear down Baal's altars, the 400 absent priestesses will flee back to Sidon, maybe Jezebel with them. What would it be like if Jezebel publicly repented, and called the nation to follow her in serving the Lord as intensely as she had served Baal? Your incredible run into the city would be a celebration of joy to the Lord.

In the triumph of that moment, Elijah was physically and emotionally exhausted; although probably, in the emotions of the moment, he was not aware of it. Although his body craved sleep, it would be out of the question.

155

It is doubtful that, having prepared himself for the confrontation on Carmel, he had slept the night before. Then came the day under the blistering sun with the enormous tensions of the day. Although completely confident of what God would do, he still would experience tremendous stress.

A concert pianist, although totally confident of his ability to perform, still goes through the energy-draining tension of actually doing it before the audience. A man may minister with ease under the anointing; but afterward, his physical body is exhausted from the stress of being before the people.

The high moments immediately following the fire leaping from heaven to the altar as the crowd broke into wild enthusiasm . . . he knew it would happen, but the actual event would be registered by every emotion in his body and soul.

Personally executing the 450 prophets drained him more than the moment allowed him to see. His clothes, covered with their blood and his arms weak from wielding the sword, would be enough to make an average man go home to bed. But Elijah is caught up in the national victory he has achieved. As he ran into Jezreel, he doesn't realize it, but he is an exhausted man.

Ahab took the news of what happened to Jezebel. Her prophets are not only lost to Elijah, but they are dead by the winner's hand. Jezebel flew into a rage and made a covenant between herself and the Baals: Elijah would die in the same way as her prophets had — within 24 hours — or Baal could kill her!

She sent a message on royal note paper to the inn where Elijah was staying: . . . **"So may the gods do to me and even more, if I do not make your life as the life of one of them by tomorrow about this time"** (1 Kings 19:2 NAS).

When Elijah read the message, his world fell apart. Like the wind that blows out the candle flame, so the words of Jezebel engulfed him in darkness in which, suddenly, nothing made sense.

The 29 words the queen's message contained spoke volumes to Elijah's tired mind. Jezebel had not responded as he believed she would. It was beyond belief that, even after the miraculous events that had taken place on Mount Carmel, she still believed in the Baals!

Obviously, she did not see the nation as having repented and turned in faith to the Lord. They had simply been momentarily overwhelmed by a show of power. In her mind, the people still believed in *Baal Melkart*, and in her authority as his high priest.

If she had believed for one minute that the nation had turned back to the Lord, she would never have sworn to have the national hero of Carmel dead within 24 hours. To her, Carmel was an irritating set-back in her plans, nothing more.

As Elijah read her message, he found himself believing that she was right. Suddenly, Carmel seemed to be a long time ago, almost a dream. A few minutes before, he had sat in the euphoria of seeing himself taking part in the celebration as the nation returned, en masse, to its covenant God.

Now, the events on the mountain appeared as a very unusual Sunday School picnic. It was all over now and life would resume as usual. The leaders he had believed to be calling on God for mercy were now calling on their guards to hunt him down and kill him.

He was devastated. What he had worked toward for years collapsed before his tired eyes. He had been so certain that the Baals would be gone forever after today; but in the light of this message, they were here to stay! Once he had entertained that thought, it opened the door to other thoughts that had been nibbling at the back of his mind for hours.

Why had the triumph turned into such a defeat? He remembered bitterly all the believers who had not stood with him. They sat around a fire in their cave tonight, praising God for the victory they had not lifted a little finger to be a part of. He raged against their cowardice and their arrogance in calling themselves prophets. They had run like roaches to their darkness when persecution came. He was the only prophet God had — "And they are going to kill me, and there will be no one left.

"If everyone who claimed to be a believer had stood with me on Carmel, Jezebel would have known the day of the Baals was over, but she is laughing at one man from the mountains of Gilead." All the pseudo believers had let him down, and left him to handle the enemy alone.

But his anger did not end with believers. Where was God in all of this? Didn't He care that His altars were broken and His people enslaved by Baal? Why didn't He remove Jezebel? Elijah felt that he was the only person in heaven and earth who really cared about the triumph of righteousness in Israel.

"I am God's only foothold that He has left in Israel, and they are going to kill me. And He doesn't do anything!" If he felt alone on Mount Carmel, he felt utterly forsaken now, as his weary mind yielded to the darkness he felt closing around him.

The torrent of negative thoughts had a grain of truth; but two days before, he would have seen the whole situation in a different light and from an entirely different perspective. To begin with, the Elijah of yesterday would have laughed at Jezebel's note, knowing that God was his shield and personal protector.

Jezebel couldn't touch God's servant without God's permission! And if He gave that permission and allowed His servant the honor of martyrdom, then he would die with triumph.

He would also have seen through her bluff. If she knew where to send the note, why bother to tell him that she would kill him within 24 hours? Why not send an assassin instead of a messenger boy? Was she staking everything on his being afraid and fleeing, so that a confrontation would be avoided?

In the darkness that had engulfed him, Elijah acted as he had never acted in his life before. **And he was afraid and arose and ran for his life . . .** (1 Kings 19:3 NAS).

Faith is a response to a revelation of God in our hearts; fear is a response to the data the five senses can glean from a situation.

With the fear, the bitterness he felt toward those who had let him down took over his mind. He left Israel to its fate at the hands of Jezebel. He had given years of his life to rescue God's people from Baal, and now he threw them aside and ran for his own life. As far as he was concerned, the apostates and the cowards deserved one another: they could all go to hell!

God's call on his life is forgotten; he must look after himself. "All the so-called believers can sit in their caves and start praying for another deliverer who will go and stand alone! This one is exiting the stage."

His servant came with him, but at Beersheba on the edge of the wilderness, Elijah wants to be utterly alone. He feels that all people are a burden to be with, they disgust him. Even the presence of his trusted servant annoys him, and he sends him away before plunging into the desert by himself.

He feels as David had felt hundreds of years before:

My heart is in anguish within me,
And the terrors of death have fallen upon me.

Fear and trembling come upon me;
And horror has overwhelmed me.
And I said, "Oh, that I had wings like a dove!
I would fly away and be at rest.

"Behold I would wander far away,
I would lodge in the wilderness."

Psalm 55:4-7 NAS

Elijah wandered in the furnace heat of the wilderness, his feet blistering in the scorching sand, utterly alone except for the snakes and scorpions that lay under the rocks. As the sun began to go down, he came on an oasis and threw himself down under a broom tree.

He hadn't slept in more than three days . . . probably since the day before Mount Carmel. In his extreme weariness he prayed,

. . . "It is enough; now, O Lord, take my life, for I am not better than my fathers" (1 Kings 19:4 NAS).

Many a burned out person has thrown himself on a bed and bitterly prayed that prayer: "It is enough, let me die!" The feeling is, there is nothing left worth staying alive for . . . death would be welcome. One person put it perfectly when he said to me, "There is nothing left to excite or inspire me, no challenges left that I am interested in rising to. I am bored with life . . . just let me die."

As he stumbled across the desert, Elijah had been looking back at the decisions that brought him here from the hills of Gilead. Now he moans that he is no better than his fathers; they were mountain men, content in the hills with their simple life.

"What craziness ever possessed me to think I could take on Queen Jezebel? What wild dream made me think I could change anything in Israel? I am a mountain man and should have stayed there. It was the greatest mistake of my life when I left home . . . but it is too late now, just let me die."

The irrationality of the burned-out person . . . if he wanted to die, he should have stayed within reach of Jezebel!

Chapter 16

THE ANSWER

TO SPIRITUAL BURNOUT

How did God heal His weary, burned-out servant? He didn't listen to the prayer that Elijah sighed Godward out of his feelings of despair. God loves us too much to answer all our prayers or listen to all the words that spill out of our mouths. If He did, the population of the earth would be greatly diminished!

God healed Elijah by revealing His grace to him as he had never before experienced or seen it. Some people are amazed as they read this account, for they find no condemnation from the lips of God.

God loved His servant back to spiritual sanity. He did not leave or forsake him. In all Elijah's wanderings over the next weeks, God walked with him. While he seethed in his bitterness and anger, God was silent in His love, waiting for Elijah to come to the place where he would be ready to hear what He, God, had to say.

If ever there was a time when we might be tempted to ask Elijah, "What might have happened if you had stayed and confronted Jezebel . . .," or to add to his despair by saying, "If only you had stayed, Israel would have been carried into a wave of revival unknown before in history . . . ." But God never speculates as our human flesh does; He lives in the pulsating *now*.

God did not even demand Elijah to rededicate his life to His service. He simply loved him where he was.

The first step of that love was to minister to the physical needs of Elijah. He desperately needed healing sleep and, as he sat under the broom tree, God not only put him to sleep, but appointed an angel to watch over him and cook him a meal!

Many hours later, Elijah was awakened by the angel shaking him, and the smell of newly baked bread and the smoke of the fire reached his nostrils. Sleepily, he ate and fell back into a deep slumber. Later, maybe after a second day of sleep, the angel wakened him to another meal.

In dealing with the problem of spiritual burnout and exhaustion, we must not forget that we are spirits who live in physical bodies. And the resurrection of the body has not yet taken place! If we abuse our bodies, through the food we eat, lack of sleep, an overloaded schedule, little or no time to rest and recreate, we can be sure that it will be reflected in our frayed emotions, dull minds and weary spirits. In His love and wisdom, God was giving Elijah an emergency sabbath rest, something that even unfallen man was commanded to enjoy!

If we are under great physical, emotional or mental strain, that too will reflect in our spirits. At such times, we must be aware of the possibility that our spiritual energy will be drained.

This is especially true of those who are involved in ministry. The mental and emotional strain of becoming deeply involved in the problems of others drains our energy and strength. Long hours without proper rest, weeks without a day to relax, sooner or later, results in living on the edge of physical exhaustion. This is when burnout can take place.

Paul points out that our human weakness is necessary so that we may constantly be showing the power of Christ in our lives. **But we have this treasure in earthen vessels, that the surpassing greatness of the power may be of God and not from ourselves . . .** (2 Cor. 4:7 NAS).

However, when we are pressured, unless we are aware of the danger, it is easy to lose sight of the grace of God. We can become disorientated and fall into the trap of drawing on our own strength — which is already operating in the red! This is what Elijah did.

After the second meal cooked by the angel, Elijah left the oasis and headed south into the desert. He wandered in the wilderness for six weeks, but it was only 200 miles to where he eventually found himself. An average walker could have covered that distance in ten days, but Elijah walked for six weeks in what Moses described as, "**. . . the great and terrible wilderness, with its fiery serpents and scorpions and thirsty ground where there was no water . . .**" (Deut. 8:15 NAS).

Through all those days and nights, one thought went around in Elijah's mind, repeating like a scratched record. At the end of his torturous journey when he spoke with God, that one thought was the first thing out of his mouth.

> "**. . . I have been very zealous for the Lord, the God of hosts; for the sons of Israel have forsaken Thy covenant, torn down Thine altars and killed Thy prophets with the sword. And I alone am left; and they seek my life, to take it away.**"
>
> **1 Kings 19:10** NAS

Six weeks after fleeing from Jezreel, Elijah still had no answers. He had not advanced one millimeter in his thinking. All he had was a complaint which arose from his bitter disappointment in people.

But in all his wanderings, he was moving toward Horeb, the mountain where God had made covenant with Israel. It was the mountain where God had given them the Law, and where Moses had beheld the glory of the Lord. It was known as the Mount of God, and this bitter, angry, self-pitying prophet found his feet being drawn in that direction.

He had known God's grace; he had walked in faith and union with his covenant God. He knew from experience that only God could answer the question in his heart . . . the question he could hardly put into words.

Finally, before him rose the majestic peaks of the Sinai. It was here that Israel had come and received the Law through the hands of Moses. And it was also the place where Moses had entered into a cave as God revealed His heart of love, when His glory passed by.

Elijah was drawn to the place where God first entered into covenant with His people, Israel. And now, after all these centuries, Elijah felt he was now the last covenant believer left in Israel . . . he needed, he thought, to know what God planned to do now.

He found a cave in which to live and sleep while he waited for God. He was not disappointed, for God spoke, . . . **"What are you doing here, Elijah?"** (1 Kings 19:9 NAS).

Again, there was no condemnation . . . just a question that was a gentle chastisement in itself. Elijah came with questions about the way God had acted, how his fellow Israelites had behaved, and why no one had responded to the demonstration of God's power on Mount Carmel. God did not wait for him to ask any question, but instead, asked one that cut to the heart of Elijah's problem.

"What are you doing here . . .?" It had the sound of mild suprise, as if He was saying, "Hello, I didn't expect to find you here!" It pointed to the fact that in leaving Jezreel, it was the first time Elijah had acted without a specific word from God.

When he first went to visit Ahab at the palace, it was because of a word from God. Throughout the drought he had been directed, step by step, through the word that came from God. The last direction he had received was that he should go to Carmel where he should have stayed until further word.

In reply, Elijah droned out the self-pity, bitterness, anger and disappointment that had been his continual meditation in the desert.

> . . . **"I have been very zealous for the Lord, the God of hosts; for the sons of Israel have forsaken Thy covenant, torn down Thine altars and killed Thy prophets with the sword. And I alone am left; and they seek my life, to take it away."**
>
> **1 Kings 19:10** NAS

In a sense, it was a correct answer. All his negative feelings were in what he said, the hurts, confusion, anger and bitterness . . . and his weariness with all of it.

The very fact Elijah had to make the statement was his real problem. All that he said was happening had been true for many years; but after the miraculous events on Mount Carmel, it should no longer be true.

He should have been reporting that his zeal had been rewarded, that the sons of Israel had repented and returned to their God en masse, and that Ahab and Jezebel had led the way in proclaiming the nation to be God's covenant people. He should have been saying that he was now one of millions of believers, and the honored hero of Israel!

But nothing had changed. "Do you hear me, God?" he asks. "Nothing at all has changed. Jezebel is acting as if Carmel never was . . . that's what I am doing here, Lord God!"

The Lord directed him outside the cave and, as he stood looking out across the ravines and precipices around him, a great wind began to howl through the mountain. It seemed the foundations of Horeb shook, boulders flew through the air carried by invisible fingers. Elijah trembled at the demonstration of power, but all he felt was awe; there was no sense of God's presence in the tornado.

Hardly had the wind died, when the earth began to reel beneath his feet. He caught onto the rock face to steady himself as the mountain tottered in the earthquake. Below him, he saw canyons open as rocks were torn apart; boulders bounced down the sides of the mountain. Again, he bowed in awed silence before the power, but God's presence was not in the earthquake.

Following the earthquake, a thunder storm unleashed its fury around the prophet. Lightning, such as he had never before seen, hung in the air and then ran along the ground. All over the mountain, trees were struck and burst into flame. Finally, the storm moved on and became a distant rumble, and Elijah knew that God had not been in the lightning fires either.

The raw power of the Creator had been demonstrated before his wondering eyes; this is what God, the Creator, can do if He wants. It was in this very fashion that He had revealed Himself to Israel when He gave the Law on this very spot centuries before. Exodus records that on that day:

> **. . . there were thunder and lightning flashes . . . so that all the people who were in the camp trembled . . . .**
>
> **. . . the Lord descended upon it in fire; and its smoke ascended like the smoke of a furnace, and the whole mountain quaked violently.**
>
> **Exodus 19:16-18 NAS**

The Law, like the almightiness of God, inspires awe, holy fear and trembling, but not the sense of Who God really is.

Elijah had thought that a display of God's omnipotence, before the eyes of apostate Israel, would change their hearts. God dramatically showed him that the presence he sought for Israel, and now for his own troubled spirit, was not in a show of His power.

Almightiness will cause a man to acknowledge that God is, but it does not describe the heart of God. Mount Carmel had showed the futility of the Baals, but it had not changed the heart of Jezebel or the people. And now, weary and exhausted on Mount

Horeb, Elijah did not need God's power, but rather His love and grace to heal him.

As the last of the thunder died away, there came a breeze, so light that it was almost imperceptible, "the sound of a gentle blowing." In stark contrast to the ravages of the last hours, the stillness was audible. In that stillness, Elijah recognized the presence of God.

In the Hebrew language, the word for *wind* is the same word that is translated *spirit*. Only the context can say whether the word is being used to describe the wind or the moving of the Spirit of God. God, the Spirit, moved like a gentle breeze, and Elijah recognized Him.

It was obvious what He was saying. He had displayed His power in the tornado, the earthquake and the storm. He had showed Elijah that He was the Creator and present controller of His universe, greater than all the gods of the pagans.

But God is not only raw power. That is how the pagans had come to invent their Baals: they had worshipped the powers they observed in creation, not realizing that they were actually the footprint of the Creator!

That Creator and upholder of His universe was love and grace. When John defined Him, he said, **. . . God is love** (1 John 4:8 NAS). He is holy, but it is the holiness of love? He is almighty, but His power is the expression of His love. When we come to His heart, He is like a soft gentle breeze rather than a tornado.

God is saying, "I am not found in watching a display of power, but by My Spirit of gentle grace working in the hearts of people." He has and is dealing with Elijah in grace, and that is the way He will deal with Israel.

Was Carmel a mistake? No! There is a time when God shows Himself in such a way that man can see the emptiness and futility of all he has believed to be god . . . so he can stand in awe before the true God. But that must be followed by the incredible revelation

167

that, now that we have discovered how wrong we are, He does not judge, but loves and will move into the heart that will receive Him.

If there is an answer to what might have followed Carmel, it is here. It should have been followed by the preaching of God's pardoning love to the stunned nation, and the calling of them to personal faith in Him.

In the gentle wind of His presence, God put the same question to Elijah that He had asked before the demonstration began, . . . **"What are you doing here, Elijah?"** (1 Kings 19:13 NAS).

For the second time Elijah gave his answer,

> . . ."I have been very zealous for the Lord, the God of hosts; for the sons of Israel have forsaken Thy covenant, torn down Thine altars and killed Thy prophets with the sword. And I alone am left; and they seek my life to take it away."
>
> **1 Kings 19:14 NAS**

In repeating the statement, Elijah was saying that he was there for the same reason, he had not changed his mind. And things were still the same, he was sure. But in the revelation of God's heart and in His method of working, all that had disturbed him was now seen in a different light. In seeing God's grace in a fresh way, Elijah saw that God had not given up on either him or the people.

"Yes, the altars are still broken down. It is a fact of history that they have killed the prophets of the Lord, and they are seeking my life . . . it is all still true. But I see now that God is working quietly, gently blowing His life into the hearts of all who will receive Him."

All the Elijahs of the world want God to change people. Deal with them in power so they will repent and ask Him for mercy; run an ad to announce how wrong they have been. Come to those they have hurt, apologize and ask for forgiveness. Elijahs always want God to unscramble scrambled eggs.

Secretly, we all want God to be the Infinite Bully, to throw His power around and make people respect Him — and us. But when He throws His weight around, it is the weight of His love and grace. He does not coerce people with power, but opens their eyes from within.

To the burned-out person who has known and walked in God's grace, the word that came to Elijah is the same. The answer to our condition is in a deeper understanding of God's grace, receiving that grace for ourselves and for everyone else.

God deeply cares about the injustice and the wrongs but, obviously, He is not shocked. He knows that His power observed will never change anyone. It is only the moving of His Spirit in the hearts of men that will ultimately bring about His will in their lives.

A person is healed of burnout when he receives a fresh revelation of Who God is. This does not make sense to human reasoning. We think that we would be healed if we could see God judging all the people who have disappointed us or, at least, making them come and tell us how wrong they were! We would be satisfied if there was a demonstration of power that ordered life in the way we feel it would show God's glory the best.

We come to God and demand a formula, a series of steps we can tell others we followed to get out of the pit of spiritual exhaustion. But God frustrates us, He doesn't give us a formula . . . He gives us Himself! Understand Who He is, and everything begins to fall into place. The answer to spiritual burnout is to respond to God afresh, and discover a new relationship with Him.

The "sound of a gentle blowing" has become flesh and lived among us in Jesus. The Gospel is that He has risen out of death and is now alive and, by His Spirit, is breathing His life into our weary, tattered spirits and making us whole.

The very first disciples are excellent examples. Their world had fallen apart. Two of them walked the road back home to Emmaus, their faces telling the story of hopeless despair. They were completely burned out — life was over as far as they were concerned. Whatever their future held, it would only be marking time until they died.

Jesus, risen from the dead, comes alongside of them. His identity is hidden from them. They pour out their misery and sum it up in the words that epitomize the burned-out person: **"But we were hoping that it was He who was going to redeem Israel . . ."** (Luke 24:21 NAS).

All their hopes were shattered. As far as they were concerned, He was dead and buried. Their own leaders had crucified Him, their own people had screamed for His blood and His best friends had run for their lives.

Then He began to give them a new perspective, revealing the heart and ways of God. The burned-out flame in their spirits was rekindled. At supper that night, He revealed Himself to them, the risen One, and was gone from their sight.

They ran back to Jerusalem to tell the others, and He was there to tell them Himself. Then He stood in front of each one and breathed Himself into them. The sound of the gentle blowing entered their lives and they were burned-out no more.

There is much advice being given today that seeks to rescue burned-out believers. It consists, for the most part, of formulas and lists of things to do. None of them work! God is not a formula, nor can our hearts be satisfied with a formula.

Many became burned-out because they lived by formulas; but it is only after there has been the sound of the gentle breathing of God's grace in your life that the advice and suggestions become valid.

With his new perspective, Elijah was ready for a new commission. It was to appoint others to deal with Baalism as Elijah never could. He was also given Elisha to train, but also to have as a companion.

But Elijah may have wondered what the gentle wind of God was doing. He hadn't seen much of it! Just as he was about to leave the cave, God told him that there were 7,000 in Israel who had not bowed to Baal.

This was God's gentle way of telling Elijah that he was not the only one left! The grace of God was working where Elijah's eyes could not see. They were not all Elijahs and they could not all take on Jezebel, but they were God's covenant people, known to Him.

Neither God nor Elijah ever brought up the subject of Mount Carmel again. What might have been is known only to God, which is true for all of us. God totally leaves the past, embraces our present, and joins us in this adventure of life.

Chapter 17

THE PROBLEM

OF UNFORGIVENESS

One of the major problems a burned-out person has is unforgiveness. Usually, it is rapidly growing into deep-seated resentment and bitterness.

A spiritually burned-out person has been disappointed on all fronts, but especially with other people. All the hopes of walking with God the spiritually exhausted person had, in some way, involved believers. And all along the route of life, he has erected markers that name the people who have failed to live up to his expectations.

When the burnout began to be manifested, there were usually bitter confrontations with others who were believers. Sometimes, we feel we can handle hurts from pagans easier than from our brothers and sisters in Christ. David explained the double hurt that betrayal by a brother brings:

> **For it is not an enemy who reproaches me,**
> **Then I could bear it;**
>
> **Nor is it one who hates me who has exalted himself against me,**
> **Then I could hide myself from him.**
>
> **But it is you, a man my equal,**
> **My companion and my familiar friend.**
>
> **We who had sweet fellowship together,**
> **Walked in the house of God in the throng.**
>
> **Psalm 55:12-14** NAS

A major step for returning to spiritual vigor and strength is to forgive all who have been part of the hurts of life. Forgive those who have failed you, who were not there when you needed them the most. Forgive the gossips who carried the news of your exhaustion and problems to every believer in the vicinity. Forgive those leaders and elders who have hurt you with their words and actions. And forgive those who you thought were spiritual giants, but were found to have feet of clay and a set of weaknesses just like everyone else.

Do not despise the Pharisee. The person who despises the Pharisee has become one! Although He confronted them so often, Jesus never held resentment against the Pharisees. He wept over the religious people of Jerusalem.

> **"O Jerusalem, Jerusalem, who kills the prophets and stones those who are sent to her! How often I wanted to gather your children together, the way a hen gathers her chicks under her wings, and you were unwilling."**
>
> **Matthew 23:37** NAS

And He prayed for those who hurried Him to His sufferings and death, **". . . Father forgive them; for they do not know what they are doing"** . . . (Luke 23:34 NAS).

Peter speaks of Jesus in His humanity, and shows us how He was able to forgive those who hurt Him so deeply. He refers to this one aspect of the sufferings of Jesus as an example that we are to follow.

. . . Christ . . . leaving you an example for you to follow in His steps,

WHO COMMITTED NO SIN, NOR WAS AN DECEIT FOUND IN HIS MOUTH;

and while being reviled, He did not revile in return; while suffering, He uttered no threats, but kept entrusting Himself to Him who judges righteously.

1 Peter 2:21-23 NAS

The Greek word we have translated *example* is taken from the schoolroom, where the child learns to write by copying under the lettering of the teacher. The way Jesus forgave is the way every believer can forgive.

Peter reminds us that when people hurled abuse at Jesus, He did not descend to their level and return it in kind. When He suffered at their hands, He did not have fantasies of their destruction and make threats of getting even.

Instead, He entrusted Himself to Him Who judges righteously. In the days when Peter wrote, the word *entrusted* was used to describe placing something that you owned into the hands of another to manage on your behalf. So, Jesus handed over all the hurts and sufferings to His Father, leaving Him to manage them, recognizing that He is the only true Judge.

When seen in this light, we realize that forgiving another person involves more than deciding to forget the past. It is at the heart of our faith in God. To forgive is to recognize that we do not have the all-knowledge that is involved in true judgment, nor do we have the love, grace and mercy to temper justice. The forgiving of another human being is the act of faith in God, that He is God and the only One Who has the right to judge.

Believing that he can be as God, man still lives in the lie of the Fall. This lie is the driving force behind his life. He pursues those who have hurt him; he demands revenge. The Law said, **. . . "AN EYE FOR AN EYE, AND A TOOTH FOR A TOOTH"** (Matt. 5:38 NAS). Man demands the whole mouth in revenge for one tooth hurt; if it were left to him, all the world would be blind!

Faith hands judgment over to the Father and, in so doing, confesses that He is the only One able to judge perfectly. The act of forgiveness is the choice to acknowledge God in a situation, opening the door for Him to work both in those who inflicted hurt and those who are now forgiving.

This reveals the true meaning of forgiveness. It is releasing a person into God's hands, choosing not to be his judge while leaving all judgment to God. To forgive a person is not to say that he was right in what he said or did to you; it is to release him from all debt you feel he owes you, and place him in God's hands.

After Jesus had been speaking concerning forgiveness, Peter approached Him and asked, . . . **"Lord, how often shall my brother sin against me and I forgive him? Up to seven times?"** (Matt. 18:21 NAS). It sounds like a step toward maturity for Peter . . . before he met Jesus, he probably had not ever seriously considered forgiving anyone! More than likely, Peter felt that to forgive the same person seven times was a tremendous spiritual achievement.

However, he completely missed what Jesus is talking about, which is God's kind of love. Peter's approach was like the Pharisee who said, "Tell me the law, and whatever it is I will do my duty and keep it." It is like a man asking how many times in a week he must kiss his wife or hug his children.

The Law is the way God's love looks when it is expressed in human society. Peter was trying to reduce love to a formula that could check off so many acts of forgiveness. Jesus response was and still is, shocking to the natural mind. Jesus said to him, "I do not say to you, up to seven times, but up to seventy times seven."

Jesus must have been smiling when He came down to Peter's level, saying, in effect, "Not seven, but if you are looking for a number, try 490!"

He was probably making a reference to Lamech, who boasted that he would avenge his enemies 490 times. (Gen. 4:24.) God's love is expressed in parallel terms. He was saying that, in effect, there would be no limit for no one is going to count 490 acts of forgiveness before calling a halt!

There is also a play on the numbers seven and ten which are both numbers of completion and perfection in the Scriptures. Jesus is saying that we are to forgive as completely as God does; and to show what He means, He proceeds to give us a parable.

> **"For this reason the kingdom of heaven may be compared to a certain king who wished to settle accounts with his slaves.**
>
> **"And when he had begun to settle them, there was brought to him one who owed him ten thousand talents.**
>
> **"But since he did not have the means to repay, his lord commanded him to be sold, along with his wife and children and all that he had, and repayment to be made.**
>
> **"The slave therefore falling down, prostrated himself before him, saying, 'Have patience with me, and I will repay you everything.'**
>
> **"And the lord of that slave felt compassion and released him and forgave him the debt.**
>
> **"But that slave went out and found one of his fellow slaves who owed him a hundred denarii; and he seized him and began to choke him, saying, 'Pay back what you owe.'**
>
> **"So his fellow slave fell down and began to entreat him, saying, 'Have patience with me and I will repay you.'**
>
> **"He was unwilling however, but went and threw him in prison until he should pay back what was owed.**
>
> **"So when his fellow slaves saw what had happened, they were deeply grieved and came and reported to their lord all that had happened.**
>
> **"Then summoning him, his lord said to him, 'You wicked slave, I forgave you all that debt because you entreated me.**
>
> **Should you not also have had mercy on your fellow slave, even as I had mercy on you?'**
>
> **"And his lord, moved with anger, handed him over to the torturers until he should repay all that was owed him.**
>
> **"So shall My heavenly Father also do to you, if each of you does not forgive his brother from your heart."**
>
> **Matthew 18:23-35 NAS**

Jesus gives this extreme example to illustrate His point. For a slave to have an interview with his lord and to be in debt to him for so much money would suggest that he held a position of very high authority.

The debt is hard to express in modern terms. One talent was equal to 6,000 denarii. An average worker earned six denarii a week; if he never spent a penny of his wages and saved all of it to pay his debt, it would take in the region of 20 years to accumulate one talent! Even if we allow that his position gave him a better wage, even a hundred times better than the average man, he could not pay off his debt in a lifetime.

We might get a better idea of how Jesus' listeners understood Him, when we realize that the annual taxes collected from all of Judea, Idumea, Galilee, Samaria and Perea only amounted to 800 talents! Jesus is describing a man with an impossible debt, a debt he could never pay. The man's plea for time so he could pay the entire debt is ridiculous. The king chose to ignore it and, moved with compassion, forgave him the entire debt.

This is another illustration of God's love and grace. The slave's only contribution was to incur the debt, and then to insult the intelligence of the lord by suggesting he could pay it off. God forgives us through nothing that we have done, and through no promise we might foolishly make concerning the future. All His dealings with us arise from His spontaneous love.

It should be noted that, if the king forgave the man a debt of 10,000 talents, it cost him 10,000 talents. Debts do not simply disappear into thin air; the king would have to take the loss and pay it himself. The cross and resurrection of Jesus is God Himself taking our debt and, in our place, paying it Himself.

In looking at how Jesus paints the characters in the story, it should be noted that the slave does not appear to be thankful. Others might say what a wonderful lord he had and what a fortunate slave he was to be forgiven, but there is no record that he said anything like this.

Jesus is showing us a man who does not understand the incredible debt that he has been freely forgiven. Has the man misunderstood the king? Does he interpret forgiveness as meaning that he must now try his best to pay it off? Did he think that the king was impressed by his offer to try hard to resolve the situation? Certainly, the way he acted towards the second slave shows that he had no comprehension of what he had received from the lord.

Jesus pictures the second slave as owing a mere 100 denarii. In today's money, it would be worth about 18 dollars. It was one six hundred thousandth of the debt the first slave had just been forgiven! At the average wage, it could easily have been paid off in a few months.

The forgiven slave seems to feel that because he is free from the king's debt, it makes him important and able to judge everyone else. Before his debtor can say a word, he takes him by the throat and begins to choke the life out of him. The response of the poor man is to use almost the same words that his captor had used a few moments before to his lord. The only difference is that this man's promise was within reason.

It is incredible that the forgiven man didn't hear the echo of his own words and, realizing how he had been treated, turn the moment into a celebration of joy and forgiveness to his fellow slave. Instead, the man who has been forgiven a debt that could never be repaid, now binds his fellow slave in jail for a debt that could have very easily been repaid in only a few weeks.

When we do not forgive a person, we are effectively jailing him! In the mind of the unforgiving person, the wrongdoer is forever locked into being the person who did the wrong. Like the frame of a video that is frozen to show a football play, so the hating individual freezes the object of hate in his mind. As far as he is concerned, the person who hurt him can never change; what that person said or did is the way he is and always will be.

In jail, the man would never be able to pay back his fellow slave. All that would be achieved is the forgiven slave can go to bed at night knowing that his demand for revenge and vengeance is satisfied. The key phrase is, **" 'Should you not also have had mercy on your fellow slave, even as I had mercy on you?' "** (Matt. 18:33 NAS).

God's act of forgiveness must cause us to give grace and mercy to all who have hurt or offended us. The resurrection of Jesus has forever changed all our relationships . . . not only with God, but with all the people with whom we walk through life.

The Judge has Himself taken the cost of our sin and freely pardoned us a debt that we could never repay. Never again can we assume the position of judge over others; instead, we pass on the compassion that has been shown to us. The epistles of Paul are even more explicit than this parable.

> **Let all bitterness and wrath and anger and clamor and slander be put away from you, along with all malice.**
>
> **And be kind to one another, tenderhearted, forgiving each other, just as God in Christ also has forgiven you.**
>
> **Therefore be imitators of God, as beloved children;**
>
> **and walk in love, just as Christ also loved you . . . .**
>
> **Ephesians 4:31,32; 5:1,2 NAS**
>
> **. . . bearing with one another, and forgiving each other, whoever has a complaint against anyone; just as the Lord forgave you, so also should you.**
>
> **Colossians 3:13 NAS**

In the parable, Jesus pictures the unforgiving slave being delivered to the tormenters. These were professional torturers who extracted the last dime from a debtor. It is a solemn fact that to hold unforgiveness towards another individual brings torment to a person's life.

Having seen God's love toward us, we can never act out of unforgiveness again, without realizing that we are sinning against the love that has made Himself known to us.

Many of the symptoms of burnout are the result of not forgiving those who have failed to come up to our expectations.

Anyone who has repented of hatred and received God's forgiveness for it, and has forgiven all those who wronged him, will testify to the torment that hatred brought.

We become the slave of the person we hate. All our thoughts are darkened with the thought of that person; his shadow is always hovering on the edge of our lives. Our life becomes soured, and anger seethes just below the surface, ready to lash out at anyone who happens to do something we do not like.

Our bitterness releases a poison into our bloodstream that seriously affects our physical and emotional health. In time, there is no energy left to enjoy life. Such people have been delivered to the tormenters; they are the walking dead. Unforgiveness hurts the unforgiver more than the unforgiven!

But there is forgiveness for the unforgiving! We can come out of the dungeon the torturer's unforgiveness creates, and be released into the world as manifestors of God's love and free forgiveness.

One of the torments that eats away in the soul of the unforgiving person is an undefined, hazy uneasiness about his own status before God. The unformed question that is nagging his spirit is, "If I cannot forgive my enemy, has God really forgiven me? Am I really right with God?"

The question arises from the foundation of our faith and the Gospel. The resurrection of Jesus from the dead is the announcement to people that all sin has been dealt with. Not only ours! **. . . and He Himself is the propitiation for our sins; and not for ours only, but also for those of the whole world** (1 John 2:2 NAS).

The unforgiving believer must face the fact that the sins of the man who sinned against him were included in the work of Jesus in His death and resurrection . . . including the sin that he chooses not to forgive. He is saying that at least one sin cannot be forgiven, but that immediately puts into question whether God has dealt with any sin. This brings up the nagging question of personal relationship with God.

181

It is our honor as children of God to forgive others on the basis of the work of Jesus. I am one slave who has been forgiven an incredible debt, and who is now extending the same pardon to a fellow slave who, by comparison, has hurt me in a trivial way.

Here is where we have our major difficulty in giving forgiveness. There is a voice within demanding that someone must pay for what has been done. The act of forgiveness seems to contradict all sense of justice; people should pay for the wrong they do!

Faith hears Jesus say, "I have paid, let them go free!" To forgive someone is not to say that there was no debt owed, nor is it saying that there was no hurt felt. It is releasing the person from the real debt in the light of what Jesus accomplished.

Stephen was being stoned to death and his last act was, **And falling on his knees, he cried out with a loud voice, "Lord do not hold this sin against them!"** . . . (Acts 7:60 NAS). *The Amplified Bible* translates it, **. . . Lord, fix not this sin upon them — lay it not to their charge!** . . . .

If it was not "fixed" on the murderers, who was it fixed on? If it was not laid to their charge, whose charge was it laid to? Stephen was not making a beautiful gesture, a death wish that was becoming to a Christian.

He was making a legal statement in that he was recognizing that the sin that was, at that moment, being committed against him, had already been laid to the charge of Jesus. It had been fixed on Him at the cross and declared pardoned by His resurrection.

Stephen's last act on earth was, by faith, to agree with the Father that the work of Jesus was enough to bring forgiveness to all, even to those who are murdering him! Many of us have known other believers who hurl their words, seeking to destroy our spirits. Forgive them, recognize that it is not laid to their charge . . . any more than your sin is laid to yours.

The slave could have forgiven his fellow slave and the entire community, many times over, and it still would have been only a faint shadow of the love that had been shown him. Jesus said that we would be a company of lovers, characterized by His *agape*, reproduced in the way we treat each other.

Chapter 18

THE FAITH TO FORGIVE

Once we return from our weary wandering in spiritual exhaustion, one of the first things we must do is acknowledge the people we hold a grudge or resentment against. Confess the sin of harboring unforgiveness against those who have hurt us.

The fact they did wrong does not justify our resentment, and we cannot forgive them until we ourselves have first received forgiveness for acting like the slave who jailed his fellow believer. And not only do we forgive in the light of the pardoning love that has been revealed in Christ, but because the Spirit of the pardoning Christ lives within us.

> **. . . the love of God has been poured out within our hearts through the Holy Spirit who was given to us.**
>
> **Romans 5:5** NAS

When we forgive the person who has hurt us, we do not look within ourselves for some strength or emotion with which to do it. We do not dedicate ourselves to give them more faith; the disciples felt forgiveness on that level could not be accomplished with the kind of faith they had!

> And the Lord said, "If you had faith like a mustard seed, you would say to this mulberry tree, 'Be uprooted and be planted in the sea'; and it would obey you."
>
> Luke 17:6 NAS

In effect, He responded to the disciples' request for more faith with "No!" The smallest faith, awakened by the first ray of light to come from the heart of God, is enough! The newest believer has seen enough to forgive his brother who has sinned against him.

This faith to forgive is released with words of command. The root of bitterness that could begin to take over a life is thrown into the sea, and the love of God flows on through our lives. It is significant that Jesus finished His teaching on that occasion with a strange story.

> "But which of you, having a slave plowing or tending sheep, will say to him when he has come in from the field, 'Come immediately and sit down to eat'?
>
> "But will he not say to him, 'Prepare something for me to eat, and properly clothe yourself and serve me until I have eaten and drunk; and afterward you will eat and drink'?
>
> "He does not thank the slave because he did the things which were commanded, does he?
>
> "So you too, when you do all the things which are commanded you, say, 'We are unworthy slaves; we have done only that which we ought to have done.' "
>
> Luke 17:7-10 NAS

When considered in the context that Jesus is teaching His disciples to forgive, the meaning of the parable is plain. When we have forgiven the worst of our enemies and walk through life forgiving all who hurt us, we have not accomplished any great thing. We have only been acting like those who are united with Jesus are expected to act!

There is one problem that at first seems to make forgiving as God does impossible. I have met many people who, when faced with the necessity of forgiving, respond with, "I can forgive, but I can never forget!" Is it possible to forget how people have treated us? Can we really have divine amnesia when our friends let us down? Will the hurt ever go away so that we cannot remember it?

When we forgive as God forgives, we do forget as He forgets. But we need to have a clear concept of what it means to say that God forgets. We must understand that there is nothing that is outside the mind of God. He is omniscient and knows all things. He never has amnesia!

When God pardons us, our sins do not leave the sphere of His knowledge; rather, He chooses not to bring them to mind. Speaking of His pardoning action in the New Covenant, He says, **. . . "for I will forgive their iniquity, and their sin I will remember no more"** (Jer. 31:34 NAS).

When He says, "I will remember no more," He is speaking of a choice. Forgetting is something that is involuntary; it is something that happens to us for many reasons. To "remember no more" is the divine choice of God concerning our sins.

In like manner, the hurtful events of life, the sins people have committed against us, need not be actively remembered. This is when the memory begins to fade and lose its power in our lives. What was potentially an open, festering wound that filled our lives with the poison of bitterness, now becomes a harmless scar.

In the parable of the prodigal son, Jesus outlines the process of how God no longer remembers our sins. In union with Christ, we can deal with each other in the same way.

We have already seen the *agape* of God in this story. Consider it again, now focusing on the choice of the father to "remember no more" his son's sins.

Having squandered a third of the inheritance and having lived among the Gentiles, finally becoming a hog herder, the filthy, unkempt son turns his feet towards home. The father, who had forgiven the boy from the moment he left, saw him when he was a great way off. He ran and embraced him, and repeatedly kissed him.

At this point, forgiveness has been expressed by the father and received by the boy. There now began certain actions on the part of the father that would bring about a relationship between them in which the boy's sin was remembered no more.

The first action he took was to order that the best robe be put on him, as well as shoes on his feet and a ring on his finger — all while they were still a great way off from the farm. The reason for the father's actions is obvious. When the son walked through the town and farm in his father's best robe, no one would know the gutter in which he had lived. That would forever be a secret between the father and the forgiven son.

If we are going remove the poison from a memory and no longer remember a hurt, we must take the position: "I am not going to bring this matter up to anyone else; it will remain a secret between me and the person I have forgiven."

In giving the boy his ring, the father took a second step. While still among the pigs, the boy had prepared a speech in which he asked to be considered as a hired servant. If the father had wanted to make him pay for his sin, this was the perfect opportunity.

In the position of a hired servant, there would be many times when he would sit in the market place with no one to hire him. He would be without money and would have time on his hands to think of what might have been. He would have looked at his father's house and remembered that he was born to be the joint owner. He would have lived in the punishing despair of his foolishness and sin.

If the father had not acted as he did, he would have looked down to the market place every day and reminded himself that his son was paying for his sin. The father would have brought the whole business to his remembrance and relived the entire scenario.

Instead, the father reinstated him as a son and gave him his ring. In those days, the ring was not just a piece of jewelry, but was the equivalent of a credit card. It was a signet ring, carrying the signature of the owner which was the guarantee of payment for any goods selected by the bearer.

In doing this, the father took a deliberate step to remove anything that would remind either of them of past hurts. To forgive in a way that the hurt is purged from his life, the person forgiving must promise himself not to bring up the matter of the forgiven sin or to remind anyone of it.

The third action the father took was in his conversation with the elder brother. When the elder brother returned home and heard the sounds of the feast, he sulked outside and refused to come inside. The father went and pleaded with him to join in the welcome home feast. The angry man is not interested in any welcome . . . all he wants to do is rehash what the prodigal has done, and the shame and embarrassment he has brought to both himself and the father.

It would have been the perfect moment for the father to indulge in a pity party with his moral son. He could have agreed with him that the younger brother had caused them both grief. To have done so would have provided the opportunity to feel condescending toward his returned son, reminding himself of just how much he had forgiven the boy. In the son standing in front of him, was a sympathetic ear that would have taken great pleasure in continuing to rehash the crimes the brother had committed against God, society and the father.

Instead of pursuing the conversation, the father gently rebuked the elder brother: **" 'But we had to be merry and rejoice, for this brother of yours was dead and has begun to live, and was lost and has been found' "** (Luke 15:32 NAS). In refusing to pursue the conversation, the father was saying that the past was a closed book and would not be discussed again.

The person who forgives and takes steps not to remember, must determine that he will never raise the events of the past, to gloat over how great a debt has been forgiven! As far as the forgiving believer is concerned, the file is closed.

Describing God's love in our lives, in relation to forgiveness, Paul wrote, (Love) (*agape*) **. . . does not take into account a wrong suffered** (1 Cor. 13:5 NAS). One translation renders it, **Love . . . keeps no lists.** This reflects exactly what the text is saying. God's kind of forgiveness does not keep referring back to the file to see how great was the act of forgiveness!

The father sealed his actions with the roasting of the fattened calf. There must come a moment in our lives when the matter is forever done. We draw a line across this day, and forgive every person above the line who has helped bring about our burnout, or who has contributed to it by his actions and words.

No one drifts into forgiving others; it is a decision followed by an act. Sometimes, forgiving others cannot be said and done to them personally, but it must be done in the presence of God, naming the individual whom we are now forgiving.

I have found that usually the burned-out person has a list of many people who must be forgiven. Do not dismiss it with, "I forgive everyone!" Bring each person to mind and, in God's presence, let your faith name the individual and forgive him for the specific hurt that he caused.

Remember, you are speaking your forgiving words in faith, and feelings will not necessarily come at once. Many times, our response of faith to Christ within us, recognizing Him as our strength to *agape*, stands nakedly on God's Word for a long time before feelings come.

Some years ago, a person did me great harm. Jealous of the way God was using me, he began to spread lies, seeking to destroy my ministry. The situation was aggravated by the fact that the person had been a close friend.

One night, it came to a head before the congregation. By this time, the matter had gone too far, and there was nothing I could do. To my limited mind, it looked as if my ministry was over. In numb despair, I walked away from the church.

I found myself on a deserted country road; it was dark all around me, and in my spirit as well. Angry, bitter thoughts raged within me. Questions went around and around in my head . . . how could he have stooped so low to do such a thing to me?

I knew resentment and hatred was being birthed in my heart. I also knew that, unless the matter was dealt with that very night, my enemy would not have to destroy me . . . I would destroy myself with unforgiveness.

Stopping on the road, I called out the name of the man who had been my friend and was now my would-be destroyer. And then, I said, "I forgive you in the Name of the Lord Jesus Christ. Father, do not lay this sin to his charge. I recognize it was laid on Jesus and put away . . . I do not hold it against him any more." I turned and walked on down the road. By faith, I had drawn my line and the matter was settled in my heart with God.

Ten minutes later, I began to feel the anger, self-pity and resentment rising in my heart again. "How could he do it?" my hurt spirit whimpered. I stopped and said aloud, "Ten minutes ago he was pronounced forgiven, the case is closed and I am not discussing it with myself or anyone again."

During the next days and weeks, many times I had to stop what I was doing and state that, in spite of the call of my feelings, I had spoken the word of faith from Christ within me. The feelings always went away, for that is all they were . . . feelings! My true self is joined as a unity with Christ, the *agape* forgiver.

It should be noted that I was not feeling warm, gushing feelings towards him. In fact, during those days I felt nothing about him and, rather gave myself to planning what the future held. Gradually, the time between the return of the negative feelings grew longer and longer until, one day, they never came back.

I can still remember those days. In fact, I can vividly relive the history of that night; but I remember it as history, nothing more. It is not resentment or bitterness, and it has no power to hurt me or anyone else.

The story of Jesus feeding the multitude illustrates perfectly how we must act in situations like this. The multitude had been with Jesus for some hours, and the disciples were anxious that some of the people might faint from hunger. Their solution was to send the people away to find food wherever they could.

Jesus threw the problem into the lap of the disciples, telling them to feed the people! Andrew brought the boy with five loaves and two fishes, underscoring the fact that this was all the food the people had among them.

At this point the exact movements of the story should be followed carefully. Having had the people sit down, Jesus broke the loaves and fishes and gave them to the disciples . . . five loaves and two fishes broken into twelve pieces.

Considering that it is a boy's lunch, Jesus was not dividing large loaves and big fish. What ended up in the hands of the disciples was a very small piece of bread and a morsel of fish. It would have sounded utterly ridiculous to their ears when Jesus told them to go and feed the people, but remember they didn't know the end of the story!

It is hard to imagine how they would have begun . . . maybe handing out token crumbs. Soon, it would dawn on them that, whatever they gave away, the same amount remained in their hands. They had in their hands pieces of infinite bread and fish! Whenever that dawned on them, they would have enthusiastically urged the food on the people, even though they could hardly feel it in their hands.

It wasn't until later that Jesus allowed them to pick up all that remained, and they felt a little of what they had actually given away.

Christ is in us, our God kind of love, and in that faith we step out and begin to give the love and forgiveness we do not feel. It is as we walk into our days, acting as if He is there, that we discover again and again that He is. It is later that our feelings catch up.

In many cases, people do not even know they have hurt you; and in such cases, you can forgive them when you are alone in God's presence. It would not be right to give them problems they didn't know they had!

Others may be continuing in the action that hurt you in the first place and, until God has worked in their hearts, reconciliation is impossible. Let forgiveness be given to them in God's presence, in the same way that the father forgave the boy long before he came to ask for it. It is imperative that you hold no unforgiveness towards them, and that you are ready for Him to bring about reconciliation.

If there is a barrier between you and another of which you are both aware, go and ask him to forgive you for the sin of holding resentment. Share that, after being in the wilderness of burnout, you are returning to life again and want to have all wounds cleansed.

There are probably some people you will never be intimate friends with, but you must always have a heart of love and faith towards them. Let the Holy Spirit put his faith in your heart for the person you have forgiven. The human tendency is to be suspicious, expecting them to act again in the way in which they originally hurt you.

The flesh does not see how God can work in their lives and bring about a further maturity in Christ. Let faith work by love; see and believe that the Spirit of Christ is working in them, even as He is in you.

We see a shadow of this when a mother takes a crawling baby and sets it on its feet with the words, "Walk to Daddy!" To a bystander who does not know the way of parents with their children, this looks ridiculous! The baby does not understand what the mother means by "walk," and it is obvious that the calf and leg muscles are not developed enough to walk. Obviously, this child will crawl forever!

The bystander's suspicions will be confirmed when the mother lets go of the child and it immediately falls down and assumes a crawling position. Undaunted, the mother picks up the child and repeats the process again and again. One day, the child walks.

Parents act as they do because they have faith in the fact that because the child is a human, he will predictably walk upright. That faith is coupled with love that gives endless patience that eventually will bring about growth in the child.

Do not let any bitterness remain in your heart. Let today be the day of receiving God's forgiveness for all resentment that has been allowed to grow in these days of spiritual exhaustion. Let today begin a new lifestyle of giving forgiveness to all who have and, undoubtedly, will hurt you.

And as your faith releases to God all who have hurt you, begin to expect that He will bring about not only your maturity in Christ, but theirs as well.

Chapter 19

THE MINISTRY

OF FORGIVENESS

The burned-out believer is actually in a position for tremendous spiritual growth. The failures, the horror of realizing his weakness and helplessness, are the threshold of a new life! This person is now in a position to take giant steps in experiencing the love, grace and mercy of God, to walk out into a new life of discovering the reality of Christ living His life in him as never before.

But the opportunity for this new dimension of growth is not only in the burned-out person's life. It is also there for all those who are around him. Everyone who touches the life of a hurt spirit is involved in the hurt. When any part of my body is hurt, my whole body is involved in the pain. In the same way, when one member of the Body of Christ hurts, those immediately around hurt too.

For those who are close to a burned-out person, it is the perfect opportunity to put faith into action. We have sung hymns and

Scripture songs that exalt the love, grace and patience of God; we have stood in awe before His incredible forgiveness.

Now it is time to act on what we have seen and believe, to actually be the grace and *agape* of God to the bruised reed and the smoking flax, to be the extended hand of God's forgiveness to the wounded and the hurt.

Our reaction to those who have dropped exhausted on the road of life is the ultimate test of our personal understanding of God's grace. Too often, our grasp of God's love begins and ends with the singing of "Amazing Grace"! When given an opportunity to actually put it into practice, we tend to put it aside as unworkable.

Faced with the failure of one of God's children, we are forced into the position of reaffirming all that we believe. We have never truly understood God's forgiveness to us until we have extended forgiveness to our brothers and sisters in Christ.

The strange fact is, we find it a lot easier to forgive our pagan neighbors than our brothers and sisters in Christ! In rejecting the charred wick of a brother, we are taking our stand with the legalists and rule-makers, against Jesus Who delights to restore these people.

Beware of the attitude that takes the position that, if only he had acted like a responsible Christian, we could stand with him. The brother has let us down and must be punished, and so we disassociate ourselves from him. We say we love him from a distance, but this, of course, is no love at all.

The battered believer in our midst forces the whole fellowship to take another look at the foundations upon which we all are accepted by God. Perhaps this is why the legalists become so angry with the fallen . . . because they are forced to see the illogic of their own position. Is anyone accepted because of zealous involvement in spiritual things? Is our welcome into God's presence based on a lifestyle that has moved into a state of perfection? Even the legalist will admit that that is not so.

We are accepted solely on the basis of what Jesus has done for us in His death and resurrection. I affirm my faith in that work when, in spite of his present behavior, I extend forgiveness and grace to my hurting brother.

If man had been left to write David's epitaph, it would have read, "Here lies one of the greatest failures the covenant people ever knew." God wrote of him that he was a man after His own heart. (Acts 13:22.) God does not stop working with the spiritually exhausted believer who is bruised in the making. David understood this and wrote his own testimony of his greatness, . . . **Thy gentleness makes me great** (Ps. 18:35 NAS).

Approaching the border between Canaan and Egypt, Abraham became nervous and his faith fell apart. He knew that Pharaoh was always searching for beautiful women for his harem. He also knew that Pharaoh would dispose of any husband who was not willing to relinquish his wife.

Abraham callously told his beautiful wife, Sarah, that Pharaoh could have her if he wanted; Abraham was not about to risk his neck for her. He instructed her to tell Pharaoh that he was her brother. In the moment when Sarah needed Abraham's support, protection and love more than at any other time, he acted the coward and forsook her. Abraham was a total failure.

But God did not forsake Sarah, nor did He forsake her lying, cowardly husband. He worked in Abraham's life and, throughout the Scriptures, Abraham is called God's Friend. What would be our reaction to Abraham if he had been a member of our church?

These failures should become open windows for the love of God to come streaming in. When dealing with the fallen around you, make sure that you are part of God's poured out *agape*.

When I see leaders and elders condemning and trampling down the fallen, I shudder in my spirit. What will it take to bring them to the helplessness that sees the grace of God? Will they be a broken reed in a year's time?

The presence of a burned-out believer gives us the opportunity to take our place in Christ and, with eyes of faith, see through the failure and realize that here is an instrument that God is not discarding. God will fashion this person into a beautiful instrument of His grace.

We should not throw out a charred flax that embarrasses us, but should join with Jesus in making this one a glorious light to the world. We must be the tangible expression of the love of God to the fallen. As those in union with Christ, we are called to be lovers, not judges of the fallen.

Consider all that God records concerning His people: the sin of David; Abraham's cowardice; Elijah's despair when he called on God to take his life; Peter's denying Jesus in His moment of greatest need.

Did God record such details in order to embarrass these people for eternity? Is the record a kind of punishment for their sins? As one legalistic associate said, "God is a tattle tale! When you fail He will tell everyone."

The truth is quite the reverse. In these shocking stories, God is quietly saying that He is not embarrassed by our failures and that His grace extends infinitely beyond our greatest hopes.

To the degree a person understands God's grace, to that extent he is called upon to be that grace to the weak and exhausted ones around him. It is not the glib, "I love you," but the being of that love to the hurt and fallen. We are actually to become the hand of Jesus that restores the battered reeds, rather than the callous hand that tossed them aside.

Jesus told the story of the compassionate Samaritan to illustrate this point. In one sense, a man who traveled alone on the road from Jerusalem to Jericho got what he asked for. It was notorious for bandits who waited in the caves and rocks above the road. The locals called it "the bloody road!"

If one had to travel the road alone, it should have been done quickly. This man was not quick enough and, after being beaten and robbed, he was left half-dead in the gutter.

In His story, Jesus has two pass by who were religious by profession. Jericho was a city set aside for the temple religious to live in, so it was not unusual to see priests and Levites coming and going along this road.

These two hurry along with their minds full of the Psalms and the Scriptures of the temple services. Both saw the man in his desperate need and chose to quicken their pace and move past the spot. "Who knows," they were probably thinking, "maybe he has been planted there; whoever tries to help him will be the next victim. Certainly, involvement in such blood and gore will take my mind off the worship of God."

It is interesting that in telling His story, Jesus chose a Samaritan to be the helping hand of love. The Samaritans were despised and hated by the Jews; the most religious in Israel shunned these people and excluded them from the possibility of salvation. Of all people, the Samaritan knew what it was to be rejected, lonely and unwanted. Those who have been wounded find it the easiest to be the channel of God's love.

The stranger in the ditch was a Jew who, if he had been conscious, would have cursed the approaching Samaritan, even thrown stones at him. The despised Samaritan becomes a vivid example of the God-kind of love as he risks his own life for a person who, in actual fact, is his enemy. He went further and shared his own first-aid kit, led him on his donkey and paid for his lodging in an inn.

Graceless religion has not changed over the years. It still leaves the wounded in the ditch. To acknowledge their existence, to do something to help someone, would upset the smooth running of the services and embarrass the Church. Are there only executioners in God's army? Is there no Red Cross?

After we have experienced the incredible grace of God, we are gentle with our fallen brethren. Paul was a man of single vision. He would have been a hard man to work with; anyone lacking total commitment was dismissed as unfit. One such was John Mark, a young lad who accompanied his uncle, Barnabas, and

Paul on their first missionary journey. For some reason, John turned back before they really got started. (Acts 13:13.)

He went back to his mother in Jerusalem. John Mark was burned out. He embarrassed his friends who had looked to him as the spiritual giant set aside to travel with the great Paul. When Paul and Barnabas returned from their tour and testified of all that God had done, John Mark would have listened with tears in his eyes. He was lonely — the "might have been" and "if only."

Some time later, there was talk of a second missionary trip. John Mark appealed to his uncle for a second chance. Barnabas was very quick to see the grace of God in the young man's life and invited him to accompany them on the next journey.

However, when Paul heard what Barnabas had done, he adamantly refused to let John Mark accompany them. His position was final: anyone who had forsaken the crusade once could never have a second chance. So great was the argument between Paul and Barnabas that they split over the issue. Paul took Silas as his travel companion, and Barnabas took John Mark and went to Cyprus.

But John Mark could not forget that he had been rejected by the great apostle. He saw himself as a useless burnout, a charred reed good for nothing. Although not in the New Testament, early Church records tell us that John Mark met with Peter, perhaps over a meal in Jerusalem. John Mark poured out his story of failure and loneliness.

I can see Peter smile and hear his rough voice, "I failed Him when He needed me the most, just a stone's throw down the street from here. I cursed and said I never knew Jesus. But He singled me out and, not only pardoned me, but commissioned me to feed His sheep."

Peter, the broken reed that now made music for His glory, the burned-out wick that now blazed God's glory out into the darkness, took John Mark and they traveled together. John Mark became one of the most successful evangelists of the early Church and later wrote down many of Peter's sermons. Today, we call that compilation of messages "The Gospel of Mark."

Meanwhile, Paul traveled the Roman Empire teaching, preaching and, also, coming to know himself, his weaknesses and his need of others. At the end, lonely and battered by life, he wrote from his prison cell:

For Demas, having loved this present world, has deserted me and gone to Thessalonica; Crescens has gone to Galatia, Titus to Dalmatia.

Only Luke is with me. Pick up Mark and bring him with you, for he is useful for me for service.

2 Timothy 4:10,11 NAS

Paul had come to know himself and his total dependence on the grace of God. As we grow in Christ and come to maturity, we see that we have no cause to boast. Left to ourselves, before God, we are all welfare cases!

Many times, the broken reed that we threw into the river as useless is the very instrument God uses to bring His grace to us in the moment of our need. Paul was battered and lonely. Who knew what that was like better than John Mark, and who could minister grace to the lonely better than John Mark?

Knowing our personal dependence on God's grace, we restore bruised reeds with meekness. Paul speaks of this in Galatians 6:1,3 (NAS):

Brethren, even if a man is caught in any trespass, you who are spiritual, restore such a one in a spirit of gentleness; each one looking to yourself, lest you too be tempted . . . .

For if anyone thinks he is something when he is nothing, he deceives himself.

In dealing with burned-out people, we come away realizing that our strength is not in ourselves but in Christ Who is our life.

When we are dealing with people who are spiritually exhausted, we must see with the eyes of faith. We must see through what appears to be, to what actually is. The incredible fact is that

Christ actually lives in the wounded believer. God is now at work in him to will and to do of His good pleasure. (Phil. 2:13.)

Paul speaks of the rock-bottom test for every believer in 2 Corinthians 13:5 (NAS):

Test yourselves to see if you are in the faith; examine yourselves! Or do you not recognize this about yourselves, that Jesus Christ is in you — unless indeed you fail the test?

Paul does not lay emphasis on behavior, but on the final test that Jesus Christ is in us and in our hurting brother. The devil is already accusing your brother, telling him his behavior does not meet the standard of God's Law and that he is out of relationship with Him.

Our attention must always be on the incredible fact that Jesus Christ actually lives in the burned-out believer and, at this very moment, is working out His wise love purposes! As healers of the hurting, we take a very deliberate stand at this point. We see through their failure to God Who, having begun a good work, will continue it to the last day.

In being the love of God to the hurt and the lonely, we must understand that they do not always look for answers. Often, our shunning and leaving them alone is our fear of being speechless before their problems.

The fact is, they know there are no neatly packaged solutions to their problems right now. What they need is to be loved by a human being with God's kind of love. This means loving them even if they are wrong, a love that says, "I don't have all the answers, but I want to be to you all that you need me to be right now."

Jesus asked for friendship like this in the moment of His greatest need. The Gospel writers describe Jesus as they saw Him when He entered the Garden of Gethsemane: **. . . He . . . began to be grieved and distressed. Then He said to them, "My soul is deeply grieved, to the point of death . . ."** (Matt. 26:37,38 NAS).

At that time, He looked for three friends to be close to Him. It was as if He was saying, "I am afraid and lonely, and I can't even explain to you what is taking place. Just be with Me while I pray this through. You don't have to give any answers, just be close and pray." And they all fell asleep! So many spiritually exhausted believers have experienced their friends falling asleep when they needed them just to be there.

Ezekiel was called on to share the hurt of his brothers. In Ezekiel 3:15, he went to the captives who sat in blank despair on the banks of the River Chebar. He was instructed by the Spirit to sit where they sat and keep his mouth shut for a week. He had no answers, but he would sit with them in their despair. Job's friends would do well to learn a lesson from Ezekiel!

As you reach out to be God's love to the spiritually weary, wounded and burned-out, be prepared for discouragement. Remember the German Shepherd at the bottom of my garden. A person who has known rejection is suspicious and unresponsive. He is afraid that the outstretched hand is a disguised club, preparing to give him another beating and public shaming.

Encourage yourself with the fact that God has put the bleeding, battered person in your path that He might love him through you. Keep loving and simply being there until every barrier is down. Sometimes to be part of another's healing, we display with crystal clarity the God-kind of love in our human situations.

According to statistics, Jerry was a very successful pastor of a large church on the West coast. The truth was he was burning out in his attempts to build his church. In the middle of his success, it was discovered that he was having an adulterous affair with the wife of one of the deacons.

The church was numbed when it was announced at a church meeting. However, it did not take most of the members long before they found their tongues and gossiped the affair all over the city.

In the midst of all of this was Jerry's wife, Lynn. She was not only hurt by what her husband had done, but also felt like the world's greatest fool in that she was the last one to know what he was doing. She stayed at home crying, ashamed to venture into the street where she would be greeted with knowing looks or someone telling her how he or she had known all about it for a long time. She made plans to divorce Jerry.

One night, she was awakened from her sleep by an almost tangible sense of God's presence in the room. Her testimony is that she experienced the voice of Jesus within her that was as real as any audible voice.

He told her Jerry had broken the covenant of marriage and according to the Law, she could divorce him. He then gave her an alternative, ". . . or you can not only forgive him as I have, but you can join with Me in bringing about his restoration."

A revelation of God's love broke over her, and she wept for a very long time. She saw how she had been freely forgiven through the blood of Jesus, and knew that Jerry had been forgiven through the same grace. Finally, she composed herself and went to the other end of the house where Jerry was sleeping.

She knelt by his bed and told him of the divine presence she had experienced, and then took his hand and said, "Jerry, I forgive you in the Name of the Lord Jesus. I want you to know that I have joined with Him to be part of your restoration."

It took time, but Jerry was restored to God and to Lynn, their marriage was healed, and today they are again pastoring a church. He is a broken reed that has been restored . . . because Lynn was given the grace of *agape* with which to become God's restoring power to him.

There are millions of hurting brothers and sisters in the Church today. You may be one of them, depleted of spiritual energy, burned out and hurting. It could be that you also know real guilt and despair. Or you may be a bystander watching one of these hurting brothers or sisters.

The call of the Spirit to both the hurting and the bystander is to rediscover the vastness of God's kind of love and His grace, and dare to walk in it. God forgives all our sins and the mistakes of our past. We accept His forgiveness, but we continue to be embarrassed by our failures; we want to hide them in a closet.

If we will let Him, in His incredible grace, He will take those mistakes and weave them into His perfect plan. And, as to our future, we are now living from the exhaustible eternal Life, Who is Christ in us, the hope of glory. (Col. 1:27.)

When we realize this is true, in our own lives and in the lives of all our brothers and sisters, faith says, "Thank You, Father, let it be so."

REFERENCES

The Amplified Bible, New Testament (AMP). Copyright © 1954, 1958 by The Lockman Foundation, La Habra, California.

The Emphasized Bible, Joseph Bryant Rotherham by Kregel Publications, Grand Rapids, Michigan.

The Living Bible (TLB). Copyright © 1971 by Tyndale House Publishers, Wheaton, Illinois.

The New English Bible. Copyright © The Delegates of the Oxford University Press and the Syndics of the Cambridge Press, 1961, 1970. Reprinted by permission.

The New Testament in Modern English (Phi). Rev. Ed. © J.B. Phillips 1958, 1959, 1960, 1972. The MacMillan Publishing Co., Inc., New York, New York. Used by permission.